Vignettes from a Year in Borneo: Local People and Conservation

by

Carol J. Pierce Colfer

Cover Photos: Background – Danau Sentarum
Top to bottom:

Author's son, 'Alan, 2nd from left, canoeing with friends, neat Bukit Tekenang

A fisher sorting his drying catch in Ng. Pengembung

Author's husband, Dudley's head, reflected in the waters of Danau Seriang, near Pulau Majang

The village of Sekolat, in the center of the original reserve, during the dry season

Reed Wadley, center, dressed up for the *gawa'* in Wong Garai

ISBN 1-4116-7759-5

Center for International Forestry Research
2006

For my mother,

Gwendolyn Marie Harris Pierce

who, with the help of my husband,

Richard G. Dudley

gave me a fuller appreciation for the natural world in which my beloved humans live.

Preface

This book tells a story. We lived in the middle of Borneo, as a family, working on the first year and a half of a Conservation Project. The book is partly the story of our personal adjustment. We found that creating a life in the middle of Borneo was not always easy---even when one member was an experienced anthropologist! We had funny, touching, enlightening, saddening experiences that seemed to bear telling.

This is also a story of Borneo's people. I hope their individuality, their personalities, feelings, likes and dislikes come across. I wanted this story to make clear their essential humanity. Forest people must be seen not only as victims and destroyers, but also as creative actors, as human beings who can contribute to finding solutions to our shared problems. This story is about real people who happen to live in tropical rainforests.

Lastly, I wanted to convey the kinds of problems that hamper significant success in conservation projects. In my view, local people are not the primary problem. External attitudes and management, along with administrative barriers to local action, are far more central. These latter issues are what drove me from my work at Danau Sentarum Wildlife Reserve (now Danau Sentarum National Park), and have incapacitated many of my colleagues who are striving to contribute to conservation goals.

At the back of the book there is a glossary, in case the many Indonesian, Melayu and Iban words are confusing; and there is a "cast of characters and organizations." Some names have been changed to protect their privacy.

Any proceeds from the sale of this book will be donated to Riak Bumi, an NGO run by local people who worked with the project described herein---and as a private contribution to The Heart of Borneo Project.

Acknowledgements

I would like to express my appreciation to a number of organizations and individuals: At the Asian Wetland Bureau, I am particularly indebted to Wim Giesen, Marcel Silvius and Enis. Thanks go to Kathy MacKinnon and Russ Betts of Worldwide Fund for Nature, who first involved me in this project; and to Pak Hermann and Pak Tony Soehartono, of the Indonesian Forest Protection and Nature Conservation Agency, for their encouragement and support. I am also grateful for the consistent support of my institution, the Center for International Forestry Research, and particularly of my boss, Doris Capistrano, for her support. Other CIFOR staff and associates who have been extremely helpful include Rona Dennis and Atie Puntodewo who helped with the maps and Gideon Suharyanto for help with layout and cover design.

Our co-workers at the Danau Sentarum Wildlife Reserve, Markan, Sahar, Sa'id, Beben, An, Rimpun, Yanti, Mawardi and Amboi provided critical local support---often working long hours, far from their families. They were wonderfully flexible in doing whatever was requested of them, offering their own insights and suggestions, and providing invaluable knowledge of local conditions and realities.

My husband, Richard Dudley, was Chief of Party on the Conservation Project. We worked together as a team, and although we worked more closely on our formal academic studies, I greatly appreciate his active support and encouragement of all my undertakings, including this one.

My biggest debt of course goes to the people in and around Danau Sentarum Wildlife Reserve. They welcomed us into their lives, and shared their thoughts, beliefs, and knowledge with us freely. Such debts cannot really be repaid.

Contents

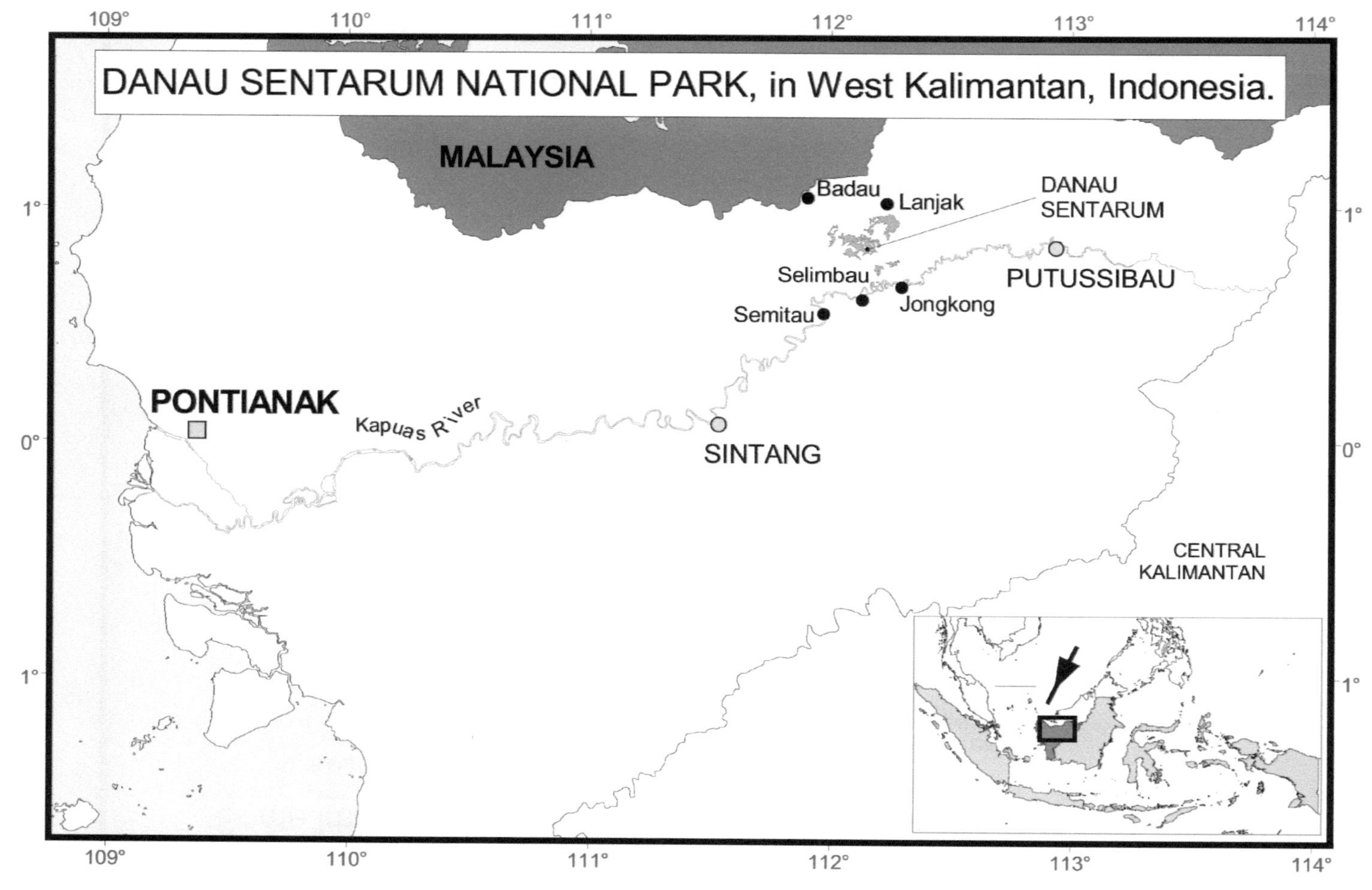

DANAU SENTARUM NATIONAL PARK, in West Kalimantan, Indonesia.
MALAYSIA
Badau
Lanjak
DANAU SENTARUM
Selimbau
Semitau
Jongkong
PUTUSSIBAU
PONTIANAK
Kapuas River
SINTANG
CENTRAL KALIMANTAN
109°
110°
111°
112°
113°
114°
1°
0°
1°

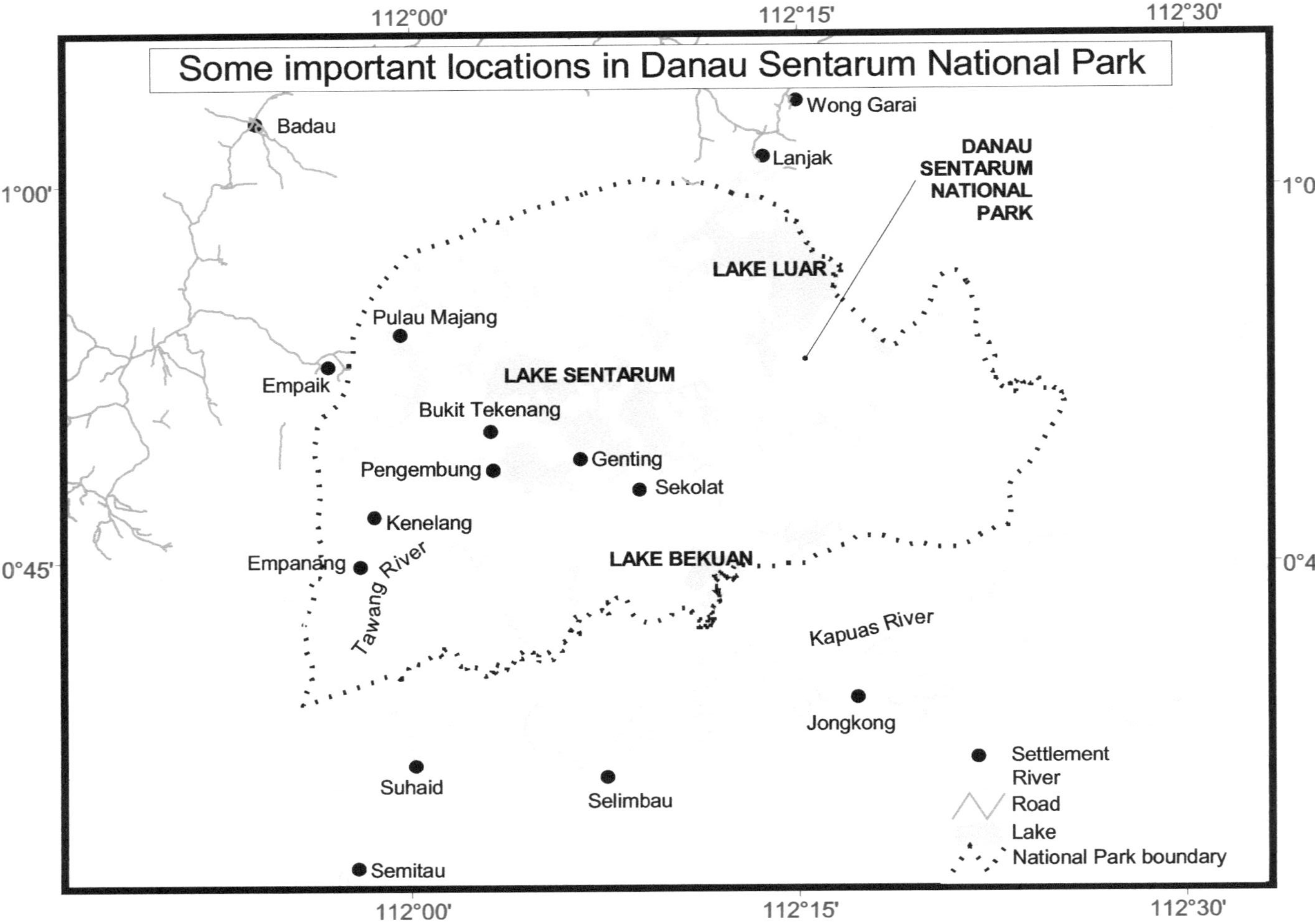
Some important locations in Danau Sentarum National Park
112°00'
112°15'
112°30'
1°00'
0°45'
Badau
Wong Garai
Lanjak
DANAU SENTARUM NATIONAL PARK
LAKE LUAR
Pulau Majang
Empaik
LAKE SENTARUM
Bukit Tekenang
Pengembung
Genting
Sekolat
Kenelang
Empanang
Tawang River
LAKE BEKUAN
Kapuas River
Jongkong
Suhaid
Selimbau
Semitau
Settlement
River
Road
Lake
National Park boundary

Chapter I: Introduction

"Gee, it's too bad ODA doesn't hire Americans," Kathy said. "There's a really great project coming up in West Kalimantan that would fit you and your husband to a T...." Kathy, a newfound ecologist friend, and I were working together on a short term consulting job in Jakarta. As she described the planned project, we agreed it sounded perfect....but...impossible, because of ODA's rule against hiring Americans. We passed on to other topics of conversation.

Some nine months later, I got a phone call from Worldwide Fund for Nature. "Are you two still interested in that project in West Kalimantan?" Definitely! So began a long wait, and---still another year later---a fascinating and challenging job. In May 1992, my husband (Dudley), son ('Alan) and I moved to western Borneo to begin to manage the Danau Sentarum Wildlife Reserve.

I was ecstatic about the opportunity from the start. We would both be employed on the same project---Dudley's a fisheries biologist and I'm an anthropologist; I could return to rural Borneo (something I had wanted to do for a long time); and I would have the opportunity to work on a topic I was very interested in: People's participation in conservation.

The opportunity to work for an NGO appealed to me as well. I had worked in many kinds of organizations---universities, USAID, the World Bank, consulting firms---and in each case I'd felt a sense of dissatisfaction. Couldn't we be accomplishing more? I expected NGO's to be staffed by idealistic people, truly dedicated to their work.

But I knew it would not be easy. The Danau Sentarum Wildlife Reserve was a two day trip from Pontianak, the only real city in West Kalimantan. DSWR was a reserve on paper only. We would be going into an area without hotels, restaurants, electricity, roads or any of the conveniences of "modern" life. I had lived in such conditions, but I wasn't sure how Dudley and 'Alan (then 11) would take to them.

The core of the reserve was unique ecologically. What, during the wet season, was a series of vast blackwater lakes, dwindled to a maze of small brown streams during the dry season. Its animal population included many endangered species. But to most people it was simply a mosquito-laden, crocodile-infested swamp! As a parent, my thoughts kept returning to the dangers to my active, outdoorsy son. I knew he was oblivious to danger and too young for me to trust fully with his own safety. And for the first time, my own and my husband's safety entered my mind. We were both 46, and had friends and relatives who had suffered from heart attacks and other ailments requiring immediate medical attention. We hoped we would remain healthy. I had many years of experience living in Third World villages, and consoled myself that we had survived plenty of other health hazards and discomforts.

As an anthropologist I was interested in the local people---Iban dayak swidden farmers and Melayu fisherfolk. Although I had worked tranquilly with Kenyah dayaks (another group of ex-headhunters) for years, the Iban are reputed to be the most ferocious of the dayak groups. There was a long tradition of enmity between the Iban and the Melayu, between the Iban and the central government, and between Indonesia and nearby Malaysia. There even remained a surprising amount of general antagonism toward the Dutch (a group into which, as *orang putih*, or "white people," we were always initially placed). Though peaceable now, the reserve was in an area with a violent past.[1]

I also recognized my own comparative ignorance about conservation. I had worked for a year (1979-80) on an ecological project, but I had never been formally associated with conservation professionals. I was committed to trying to integrate findings from my own discipline into the field of conservation. But I knew the difficulties and challenges of working with people in a new profession. Assumptions about goals, strategies, even vocabulary differ from discipline to discipline. I knew I had a lot to learn. But I reasoned that the knowledge that it would be difficult, combined with my experience overcoming such difficulties with educators, agricultural scientists and medical practitioners in the past, would serve me well. I also looked forward to applying my familiarity with people's use of their natural resources in other areas of Borneo in this new context.

---

[1] Violence reared its ugly head again in this province in the late 1990s---though further to the West.

The opportunity for my husband and me to work together was a boon. We'd already experienced ten years of following one another around, with the "trailing spouse" having to find whatever was available. Although we had managed to remain professionally active during those years, we were grateful for the chance to be doing something we both wanted. We had some misgivings about working so closely together, but felt that the positives definitely outweighed any possible negatives. We were ready to go!

Chapter II: Preparing the Way

As with many international projects, our starting date kept getting moved back, and we wound up doing several consulting jobs before we actually met our future employers. I was surprised at a November 1991 meeting where I expected to renew my friendship with Kathy and other Worldwide Fund for Nature acquaintances. We were interviewed instead by personnel from a completely different organization, Tropical Lowlands Institute. Over the next few months, WWF's role in the project dwindled precipitously.

We learned how the project was to be structured at that meeting. The Indonesian Government was the sponsor of this project on sustainable forest management. They had promised to be intimately involved throughout, supplying from four to twelve counterparts to work with us in the reserve. The British Overseas Development Administration (ODA) had given a contract to a Scottish consulting firm, SCF, for the overall project. SCF in turn had been required by ODA---apparently rather unwillingly---to sub-contract the small conservation component to the Dutch-dominated Tropical Lowlands Institute (TLI). In early 1992, while the details of the sub-contract were supposedly being ironed out, the discord between SCF and TLI was already apparent.

SCF was a large, profit-oriented consulting firm. The Project Coordinator, Jives, was suave and sophisticated, perfectly groomed, impeccably dressed, and oozing charm in urbane, social and bureaucratic contexts. I betray my biases when I say he appeared to be a good representative of "neo-colonialism." TLI was a small NGO, with a cadre of committed conservationists. Wim, our project officer at TLI, was an ex-hippy who had abandoned his earring some years back under threat of expulsion from Indonesia, but had otherwise retained much of that demeanour. He was comfortable with fieldwork, science, and very casual attire.

That the two leaders', and their respective organizations', philosophies, operating strategies, and preferences were usually in sharp disagreement became increasingly apparent as our involvement in project planning proceeded. There were disagreements and mutual recriminations about the equipment list for the project (on which Dudley and I had both expended considerable volunteer time) and about the procedures for hiring us. There were also more substantive differences. LTI, for instance, was much more concerned about the issues pertaining to wetlands, with SCF arguing for an emphasis on forestry issues.

As we began to negotiate our contracts with TLI in March and April, I found some of their attitudes worrying too. Why were they unwilling to explain their rationale in determining our salaries? Was the heavy-handed, authoritarian tone to their faxes something that would continue throughout the project? Was it a difference in Dutch and American operating styles? Although when we brought up the issue, we were assured that most project decisionmaking would be ours; I wasn't completely convinced. Maybe it was just a translation problem…

I did begin to wonder, though, if I was getting into a very congenial work environment. I sensed a real suspicion of social science input at TLI---though I couldn't quite put my finger on it, and thus had no clear way to combat it. At one point I suggested that TLI include funds for team building in their contract negotiations with SCF. Our team was to include at least two or three highly trained British volunteers (extension/education, fisheries and wildlife), ourselves (anthropology and fisheries/ecology), and four to twelve Indonesian counterparts (nature conservation), plus an undetermined number of short term consultants with varying backgrounds. I knew that getting an interdisciplinary and multicultural team to work together is difficult, but it would be critically important to the success of the project. Although I had considerable experience coordinating this kind of training and cooperation, the idea was given no credence whatsoever.

Still another rather fundamental issue surfaced. Our minor concerns about working together were doubled when both SCF and TLI---in one of their few points of agreement---refused to consider our request to share the duties of Chief of Party. They said that we could divide up the work however we wanted on site, but one of us (my husband) had to be ultimately responsible. This was problematic given our egalitarian marriage, and made us both uncomfortable. I found it professionally disappointing, since I too was qualified and experienced at leading projects; and I felt they were making it difficult for us to make best use of our respective (and very different) skills. This decision also made me wonder both about possible sexism in the organization (which was definitely ruled by men) and the priority they might or might not be giving to people's involvement in reserve management. But....in the end, we decided these were simply inconveniences we would have to accept. It would be more difficult but I thought we could manage it. Still my initial wholehearted enthusiasm for the project had begun to wane a bit.

We moved to West Kalimantan in May, where we were joined by Wim and Enis, both of whom worked for Tropical Lowlands Institute. Wim had been instrumental in having the Danau Sentarum Wildlife Reserve selected for this project, and he had written an excellent ecological report on the area based on his own fieldwork there. We were impressed with his ecological knowledge, his obvious linguistic skills, and his general intelligence. We were relieved that we also enjoyed his company. Enis was a very capable and likable young Indonesian biologist, anxious to get involved in ecological research. She was to handle financial and logistical arrangements for our introductory trip upriver to Danau Sentarum Wildlife Reserve.

I personally doubted that we would be able to make the trip at that time, because the national election campaign was in full swing, a time when foreigners are not normally encouraged to roam the countryside. 'Alan's tutor, Sarah, had agreed to look after him in Pontianak if the trip should come about.

Surprisingly, the plan continued to take shape. If Pak Toto, the head of the Indonesian Conservation Agency (CA) in West Kalimantan, could pull this one off, he would definitely gain a few brownie points in my book. Pak Toto and two of his assistants, Pak Polmer and Parto, were to accompany us on our first round of visits to provincial, regency and county officials. We would fly to Putussibau, the regency capitol, to explain our presence and our goals to the powers that be. There we would be met by our brand new speedboat, which would take us back downriver to the Danau Sentarum Wildlife Reserve, where we would meet with county officials---and get our first look at our new home!

We Meet an Orangutan

Pak Toto, who arranged our flight from Pontianak to Putussibau, warned us of the possibility of cancellation: Bad weather regularly grounded these small, 8-passenger planes. But the gods were with us, and we got off as planned. Even my usual pre-flight trepidations couldn't quell my excitement to be on my way, an excitement that increased as we flew over the wide, meandering Kapuas River. It looked just like "my" beloved Mahakam River in East Kalimantan, winding through the surrounding greenery. The predominance of oil palm and rubber plantations was not a surprise---since I'd flown in West Kalimantan before---but the same dismay surfaced. The idea of the complex and beautiful tropical forests being systematically replaced by orderly, but sterile tree crop plantations is not a pretty thought.

Pak Toto had somehow arranged for the pilot to stray a bit from his flight plan, so that we could take air photos of the Danau Sentarum Wildlife Reserve. I kept my fingers crossed that the cloud cover would not interfere. As we flew further inland, the proportions of plantations dwindled, and I could see the patchy areas where shifting cultivators lived within the forest cover. Finally, wildly snapping pictures all the while, I got my first, dramatic view of the lakes and surrounding countryside. Beautiful! There were winding rivers, vast expanses of water, forested areas some of which had intriguing, absolutely straight aquatic paths through them. Wim noted with dismay an increase in the extent of burned areas, compared to his last visit.

After we'd passed the reserve, I noticed Pak Toto looking nervously at the pilot who in turn seemed to be perusing his maps very studiously. We had flown into the cloud cover by this time, well on our way, I assumed, to Putussibau. I wondered idly what was going on, but tried not to dwell on it. I'm nervous in small planes under the best of circumstances. As we came out of the clouds near Putussibau, we learned that the pilot had in fact temporarily lost his way while flying over the mountains. I was very glad I hadn't known at the time.

Putussibau is the administrative center of the whole Regency (*kabupaten*) of Kapuas Hulu, and I was curious to see it. But our first few days there were not very satisfying. We wandered around in a group, waiting in offices for officials who never came. They were campaigning for the government's party, Golkar. Sometimes we talked with lower level officials, but they were not authorized to make decisions. We were generally frustrated.

We entertained ourselves in the afternoon hours by wandering around the market. Set out along nicely appointed boardwalks, it was an interesting place to pass the time. There were colorful vegetables, artistically arranged to appeal to passersby. The multitudinous varieties of fish, neatly laid out by species, were a special fascination for my husband who happily identified those he knew, and began the long process of figuring out the many he didn't know.

At one house, not far along the boardwalk, a woman beckoned our whole group---including the head of the province's Conservation Agency---up onto her porch. We were surprised to have our attention directed to two captive baby orangutans! She then invited us inside where she had quite a variety of other animals for sale---many on the endangered species list.

Pak Toto and I had already had several long conversations about how to begin clarifying to local people that capture and hunting of endangered species was prohibited. He seemed to understand the importance of going slowly on enforcement. I needed time to understand local people's views and behavior with regard to wildlife---something we considered very important in designing management strategies appropriate for the place and people. Partially in deference to my needs, Pak Toto had not worn his official Conservation Agency uniform.

I watched with baited breath to see how he would deal with this situation. Although Putussibau would not be in our immediate vicinity, still his response to this difficult dilemma would give me an idea about what I could expect from him in the future. He began slowly and gently to explain the new law to the people: The new law, which would go into effect the following month, specified a fine of Rp. 10,000,000 (about $5,000, at that time) for capture or killing of endangered species. I let out my breath. He had genuinely taken my point---or it had fit well with his own perspective.

However, I was almost immediately startled out of my reverie. The husband of the orangutan owner had appeared and begun to argue rather rudely with Pak Toto. It quickly became apparent that the husband did not understand that he was conversing with someone with a great deal of authority within the Province. Indeed, Pak Toto could quite legally have seized the orangutans then and there, and sent the owners off to jail. The fact that he in effect swallowed his pride and put up with this unfair abuse earned him my undying respect and gratitude.

Our New Speedboat

Our recurrent lack of success in meeting with local officials was disappointing---they were still out campaigning---and we were getting bored. While we were waiting we heard of a ceremony at a Dayak village an hour and a half upriver, which everyone assumed I would be dying to see. The perception that anthropologists are primarily interested in ceremonies is a bit of a bother for me, since under normal conditions, I do not find them that exciting---particularly so in a village about which I know virtually nothing. However, under these circumstances, I was quite ready to go see anything.

After considerable discussion and haggling, we hired a boat to take us up the river. When we got to the village in question, we learned that someone had just died. These Taman Dayaks, like many Bornean groups, have a custom that precludes anyone from entering or leaving a village for a few days after a death. Someone in a passing canoe suggested we go just a wee bit further upstream to Melapi, the next village. Although they weren't having a ceremony, we could at least see their 27-door longhouse.

On arrival at Melapi, someone met us at the riverside and took us up to the longhouse, where I put my camera to my eye to take a picture of the longhouse. But my action was interrupted by a very emphatic voice telling me that no pictures could be taken of them or their village. This was a great surprise to me since in most parts of Indonesia people beg you to take their picture. After some discussion, I learned that an earlier group of visitors had taken lots of pictures, and then printed them in a magazine story which emphasized the ignorance and primitiveness of the people. Although I had not heard this kind of story before, I was not surprised. I often feel the injustice of remarks made by other Indonesians about Borneo's people. Community members were rightly insulted and determined to prevent a recurrence. They finally relented enough at least to let me take pictures of their beautiful beadwork.

As time passed, we all began to anticipate the arrival of our speedboat ever more eagerly. Wim had not been back to Danau Sentarum since 1986, and was looking forward to renewing his friendships in the Lakes area. We were of course anxious to see an area where we expected to live for four years. On the day scheduled for the speedboat's arrival, we began checking the waterfront regularly, looking for the bright orange hull we had ordered in Pontianak, trying to see as far around the first bend in the Kapuas River as we could. We watched all day long, our eagerness (and disappointment) growing with each passing hour.

Day turned to night, and our unusual group continued to lurk on the small, covered wooden deck perched on a hill above the "port." It was about ten PM and I was ready to give up; but the group decided to wait for one last light approaching from downriver. Word came up from the water's edge that it might be ours. It *was* ours!

Pak Polmer and a driver emerged, exhausted but still smiling, from the long--and at night, dangerous---trip from Sintang to Putussibau. Floating logs, plainly visible in the daylight, become hidden torpedoes at night, poised to pierce the hulls of drivers whose attention drifts even for a second. Finding a driver in Sintang had proved to be more difficult than anticipated. We all retreated to the clean but starkly appointed Forestry Guesthouse where we were staying, and fell into a welcome sleep.

The next morning, Dudley and I expected to rise early and get underway before the sun got too hot--knowing we'd be thoroughly exposed, both from above and below, riding down the river. But our team seemed in no hurry. We lingered over breakfast, took quite a while getting everyone's gear to the riverside, and saying our goodbye's to people we had met. By the time we had everything stowed and were ready to get underway, it was well after 9 AM. Still, I thought, we're finally ready to go. We'll get to see Jongkong, the first of the villages on the Kapuas closely linked to the Wildlife Reserve, in only about four hours!

Six of us---Wim, Enis, Polmer, Parto, Dudley, and me---began clambering into the six-person speedboat, beside and behind our driver. Hmmm, a tight fit. They put Dudley and me---two of the three large ones---in the front by the driver so we could see better. Wim, perhaps 6' 2" in height, wound his tall frame into as small a space as he could in the back, with the other three relatively tiny Indonesians squeezed in beside him.

I began to have my doubts. We'd be riding like this all day for nearly two weeks....every day. Not a nice thought.

At last Polmer pulled the engine cord, and the speedboat got under way. Well, sort of. It began to move, and it gradually picked up a little speed. The driver told us to stand up in front. We did. A little more speed. Polmer climbed up to the bow; we rearranged the baggage; we swore at all inanimate objects. Nothing worked. We were still slogging slowly through the water, like a pig wallowing in a trough. To make a long story short, this continued for eight loooong hours---legs cramped up under our chins, bums numb from the incessant vibration. We gradually moved with the current down the mighty Kapuas.

The Kapuas is Indonesia's longest river. Like many Bornean rivers it is a brown, muddy color. The riverbanks provide various scenes: sometimes forest, sometimes ricefields, sometimes rubber orchards. We passed small villages from time to time. Tiny rafts lined the banks of the river, with wooden houses higher up, out of flood danger.

The river traffic was the most interesting. We were still intrigued by the *bandung*s. These large commercial vessels which looked for all the world like floating warehouses, constantly ply the Kapuas, some bringing people up and down river, others bringing goods. *Motor*s, similar but smaller vessels on which people lived and conducted small scale trade, were even more common. Some carried valuable live fish (like *kedebu', Oxyeleotris marmorata*, or *toman, Channa micropeltes*) to Pontianak in their water-filled holds. Others carried forest products downriver, and trade goods upriver. *Longbot*s, typically about 4-5 m long and a meter wide, carried people and their baggage, timber, or anything else that needed transport, usually from village to village. We occasionally saw another speedboat like our own---owned by a timber company or a trader in exotic freshwater fish, like *ulang uli (Botia macracanthus*), from the Lakes area. Speedboats were often called *bodi terbang*, which means "flying hull."

Men, women and children, in traditional canoes could be seen fishing or simply paddling to and from their fields, near any village. I remember seeing one woman, in her distinctive wide-brimmed sunhat, checking a gillnet. Her brown hands held up the fishnet, waterdrops making it shimmer in the sunlight, as she turned to see who or what was making waves in her river.

When we finally arrived in Jongkong, we were exhausted, and I wondered where we would stay. We had gone about halfway through the village which straddles the Kapuas, when Wim asked the driver to turn around and go back past a *motor* which was under construction. As we neared the *motor*, Wim called out in an inquiring voice, "Pak Markan, Pak Markan?"

Markan

A small, wiry man came out smiling and waving at us. We docked the speedboat, and Wim managed to unwind himself. He climbed from the boat onto a tippy raft, picked his way across a narrow plank, and thence to a second tippy raft where he could finally reach Markan. The two friends shook hands with obvious fondness. Markan had owned and operated the *motor* from which Wim had done his work in 1986. They had lived and worked in very close proximity for more than six months.

They made an odd pair standing there on the raft: Wim was about 6'2" with blue eyes and fair skin. Markan, about five feet tall, had the usual swarthy Indonesian complexion and twinkling black eyes. The one commonality they shared...besides their friendship....was being bald.

We were immediately invited to bunk at Markan's house, an invitation we gratefully (but somewhat naively) accepted. To get to his house, we moved the speedboat back upriver a short distance, and tied it up. We got out of the boat onto a raft made up of fish cages containing *toman* and *jelawat* (*Leptobarbus hoevenii*). The fish were jumping around in the cages, and the cages tipped a bit whenever anyone stepped onto them. The path from the fish cages up the bank to the house was a series of planks and logs on which one balanced with care. One wrong step, and a person could get wet.

One of the requirements for this job had been a medical certification that I could work in remote areas. The certification, typed by a non-English speaker, actually said I was qualified "to walk in remote areas." Seemed suddenly more relevant!

Markan's wife, mother and children greeted us with enthusiasm and interest, crowding around. Enis asked them for a glass of water, using the standard Indonesian term, *air putih* (lit., "white water"). A little while later, they came back with weak milk. It was months later that we learned that in the Lakes area *air mati* (or "dead water") is used for drinking water, not *air putih*; they could only surmise that she must want milk.

I was so tired from the long day in the sun, I wanted nothing more than to lie down and sleep---after a little food and a quick bath in the river to cool off. Markan's wife prepared what we would later learn was a typical meal (rice and boiled fish). I forced my weary bones down to the riverside to bathe, and then came back, ready to fall asleep on the hardwood floor.

I hadn't reckoned with three factors: The heat, the smell, and the mosquitoes. We opened the windows (against the advice of our hosts) in hopes that a little cool air might come in. But this let in the smell of the fish drying all along the village walkway. It also let in even more mosquitoes. I spent an almost sleepless night, alternately covering myself up to protect against the mosquitoes and uncovering myself to escape the oppressive heat. I kept remembering my query to Wim before we left: "Do I need a mosquito net?" "No, I don't think so," said he. I discovered that he had one and hadn't used it! Maybe Dutch blood is less tasty than American.

By the next morning, we had managed to send our temporary driver and one of our team members home. This would lighten the load in the speedboat considerably, and make our passage a good deal faster. We also managed to secure the long term services of Markan---who proved to be an invaluable help in almost every way imaginable. He had worked with foreigners before; he knew the plants of the reserve; and he knew the lakes area inside and out. I also bought a mosquito net.

Where to Put our Field Center

Besides visiting the five *camat*s (rather like mayors) who shared jurisdiction over the Danau Sentarum Wildlife Reserve, we would finally get to see the beautiful Kapuas Lakes...and select a location for the future Danau Sentarum Wildlife Reserve Field Center.

We first entered the lakes area from Jongkong, going up a series of small rivers toward Lake Bekuan, where we finally saw the blackwaters we had heard so much about, churning up a wake the color of tea behind us. On either side of us was lush foliage, tendrils hanging into the river, convoluted tree trunks, a panoply of greens shading us from the sun. On that first day, we saw the famous monkeys (*Nasalis larvatus*)---called *monyet Belanda*, or "Dutch monkeys," because of the males' very large pendulous nose---swinging in the branches above these small rivers.

We passed through a vast area of inundated grasses, then through small lakes and large lakes, and natural and human-made aquatic pathways of every description. It was beautiful, varied, and intriguing.

But as the day wore on, the weather got hotter. We all got stickier, and increasingly aware of our still cramped positions. And I began to get hungry. Our breakfast of ramen noodles had been hours ago.

I worried about my husband who, even under normal conditions, has an unusually large personal space. I knew he found this constant togetherness distasteful, to say the least. Reducing our numbers by one still left six people and all our baggage in the small speedboat. And we still couldn't attain normal speed.

By mid-afternoon we had reached Pulau Melayu, an island in the northern part of Lake Luar, one of Wim's candidate locations for the Field Center. While examining this small lump of land, we took the opportunity to take a quick dip, hoping for a little respite from the burning sun. I quickly donned a sarong, and started into the water. What a surprise. The temperature---which we measured---was 32 degrees centigrade! Even more intriguing was the color of our bodies through the blackwater. We looked orange. Even in the enervating heat of the water, I was grateful for the chance to get my body in motion. But we quickly rejected Pulau Melayu as a site for the Field Center. It was too small to build on and had no resident population.

Next stop was Lanjak, a predominantly Iban village on the northeastern border of the Reserve. It had been recommended by an earlier project planning team as the best location for the Field Center, and I was partial to this idea because of my interest in the Iban. The center of the village was a few hundred meters up a muddy road. As we traversed this path, the fact that each step was more difficult than the last finally made its way into my consciousness. I looked down at my feet. They were mired in about three inches of muddy red clay!

But hunger drove me on. I was sure that in a village this size there must be someplace to get something to eat. I persevered, dragging my colleagues (who didn't seem as addicted to food as I) along with me. We walked all around these muddy roads, having to stop every few meters to scrape the mud off our feet with a stick. Eventually we found a couple of possibilities----both closed! After all, we had arrived after the normal lunch hour and before dinner time. Meanwhile I realized with some dismay that my husband's impression of this Iban village was deteriorating.

We were invited by a friendly but dignified old man completely covered in intricate tattoos to stay at his house. He turned out to be the *temenggung*, the highest traditional Iban leader in the area. I declined with genuine regret, realizing that Indonesian government etiquette required us to stay with the *camat*.

Staying with the *camat* was less exotic than staying with the Iban leader would have been, but it may have been more comfortable. A few hours later, after suitable formalities, we found food, beds, a bathroom, and very few mosquitos. I was grateful not to have a repeat of the previous night!

I liked Lanjak as a Field Center site. It straddled Iban and Melayu country, which would allow me to study both systems relatively equally; and it was the site I had thought we would be selecting, based on the earlier planning team's recommendation. On a more personal note, I expected to find Dayak culture to be more simpatico with my own worldview and values. My son's biological father was a Dayak---though a Kenyah, not an Iban---and I thought it would be a wonderful opportunity for 'Alan to be exposed to that part of his heritage. On the other hand, this very personal consideration obviously shouldn't be a major factor in the selection of a Field Center site. It was becoming increasingly obvious that my interest in Iban effects on the reserve was not shared by LTI (though I knew SCF shared this interest). A real problem with Lanjak was that during the dry season it was sometimes accessible only by walking some six hours. This would mean access to supplies and communication with the outside world would also be extremely difficult or impossible.

The other team members were not taken with Lanjak. We went on to Pulau Majang, which---if living in an Iban community was out---was my second choice. This village of some 700 friendly inhabitants was clean and well maintained. There was a "hotel" of sorts, a generator which made ice for cold drinks, and a pier off which one could bathe while enjoying the sun casting a lovely light over distant mountains.

But we were gradually realizing that this trip was something of a formality, that Wim had in fact already selected the location---Bukit Tekenang---and was not really willing to budge from that choice. My job was to work with communities, and to do that properly I needed to live in one. We also wanted our son to have access to playmates, since we expected to be there for years. Bukit Tekenang's "community" consisted of perhaps ten homes on rafts, most of which were empty and/or without children!

We inquired about possible problems gaining access to the land we would need for the Center. “No problem,” said the head fisherman. The land belonged to the *kecamatan* (county or district), and this community really only fished there. I remained mildly skeptical about this, since cassava and other domesticated plants were obvious on the lower slopes of the hill.

After Bukit Tekenang, we headed down the Tawang River to visit Nanga Kenelang and Nanga Empanang---two more possible Field Center sites. In the former, we found Pak Sahlan. Pak Sahlan, we later learned, had been a famous crocodile hunter only a few decades earlier. When he learned of our interest in wildlife, he showed us a captive crocodile. The creature, perhaps two meters long, was squashed into a floating box of less than 1.5 meters. Pak Sahlan, who was later to feature in one of our community newsletters, also brought out a 1989 photo of a much bigger, freshly killed crocodile.

At Nanga Empanang, we found a very loud band playing rock music on an improvised stage in the community's soccer field. The whole village was decorated in bright colors with campaign paraphernalia littering the area as well. The field itself was full of people, many of whom wanted to have their pictures taken with us. But no one in our team seemed to favor putting the Field Center at either Nanga Kenelang or Nanga Empanang, so we resumed our debate over the relative merits of Lanjak, Bukit Tekenang, and Pulau Majang.

Wim's concern, also legitimate, was that the Field Center should be a quiet place for scientists to work. Indonesian communities are almost by definition not quiet. Privacy is an alien concept; being *ramai*, or lively, busy, active, is what makes a good community in most

Indonesian eyes. Dudley and I reluctantly came up with a compromise: We would live on a boat which could be moored at any accessible community, and commute to Bukit Tekenang. Months later we discovered---to our surprise---that Wim had thought Dudley would live at the Bukit Tekenang Field Center and 'Alan and I would live on the boat somewhere else!

Slippin' and Slidin'

The time we had allocated for this trip was drawing to a close. I was privately chomping at the bit to get back to Pontianak---from fatigue, lack of privacy, and inadequate food as well as my son's approaching birthday on May 28th. I was relieved when on the morning of the 26th Wim agreed that it was time to head back---just one more brief visit in Semitau. There we would meet the *camat* and visit the new field office that CA had just completed.

Our early afternoon visit to the *camat* was true to form: He was away campaigning, but the CA office was available for viewing. An attractive building upriver from the center of town, its main problem was that it had no access to water. Again, as we slowly and very thoroughly inspected this small building, I worried about the time. Wim seemed to be dawdling. As I understood it, we had a four hour ride---under normal conditions---ahead of us just to get to Sintang. Didn't he remember how slowly our boat moved?

My desire to get underway conflicted with my eternal hunger, and the latter definitely won out when I saw the culinary delights put before us at Semitau's most elegant floating restaurant, the Jasa Kapuas (lit. "Merit of the Kapuas"): Bowls of soup with bits of chicken and green vegetables, fried chicken, boiled eggs spiced with chillie, fried mixed vegetables, a---comparatively---endless array of items to delight the palate after days of rice, boiled fish and ramen noodles. We porked out.

To my subsequent dismay, however, it was about 4 PM when we finally got underway---ensuring hours of dangerous night-time traveling. We repeated the now familiar routine of loading up our baggage and squeezing all six bodies into our speedboat, and headed sluggishly down the mighty Kapuas. After hours and hours of nerve-wracking travel in the dark, we regretfully concluded that we had better stop en route.

Ng. Silat sports another small, floating hotel, where there was room for Dudley and me to have our own private room---our first for days. And we learned that we could go by land from Ng. Silat the next morning. It would be a lot faster. Great!

Dudley and I shut our door, snuggled down into our double mattress on the floor, protected by a mosquito net---with no loud music blaring in our ears---and fell asleep. The next morning we woke up comparatively rested, and came to the joint and spontaneous decision that a little, quick amorous activity might be in order. When we decided to rise only a short time later, we were amused and chagrinned to note that someone had opened our door between start and finish. We never were sure who had caught us *en flagrante*.

After a quick morning breakfast of the usual ramen noodles, we headed across the river where we were to board a mini-bus which would take us to a transmigrant community where we could in turn get a larger bus to take us to Sintang. Sounded easy.

The empty, waiting "mini-bus" turned out to be a tiny, dilapidated, old pickup with a covered bed and benches along the inside. Remembering that Indonesian public transport is usually crowded, I quickly settled myself up toward the front of the pickup bed to wait. We waited. And waited. And waited. We were waiting first for more customers, and later for the muddy road to dry. Finally, after a couple of hours had passed, someone decided the road was dry enough. The tiny truck was brim full; There were even two people lying on the top, clinging to the empty window frame!

My relief at getting underway quickly changed to dismay, then to fear, and finally to terror. The road we were traveling---composed of bright red mud---was as slick as glass. Furthermore, the topography of the land was mainly vertical. As we approached the foot of each new hill, the driver would pick up speed, tearing down one hill in hopes of making it to the top of the next. In most cases, this was impossible.

Since the brakes were also not in top operating condition, one of the passengers would leap out, whenever the truck began to grind to a stop, and quickly insert blocks of wood behind the wheels---to prevent us from rolling back down the precipitous incline we had just ascended. Meanwhile the danger of slipping off the road's surface was recurringly obvious, as we shimmied and jived from one edge to the other.

My chosen location in the front of a packed pickup gave me the worst of all possible worlds. I could see clearly what lay before us through the window in the back of the cab, and I knew there was no way that I could possibly extricate myself should disaster---which seemed perpetually imminent---strike.

Through the good graces of whatever gods may be, we survived. Having to wait for a couple more hours in the searing heat of a nearly deserted shop "nestled" in miles of barren, cleared land, uncertain if another vehicle would ever pass over the ribbon of pavement before us, was a piece of cake after that ride. Although we were eventually picked up by a bus and taken to Sintang, I vowed to stick to river transport in the future. But at least we made it back to Pontianak in time to celebrate 'Alan's 11th birthday.

Back in Pontianak

Although this first trip was necessary, and we certainly were interested to see our new home, it had been exhausting. Every day involved hours and hours of riding, squashed together, vibrating our way across waterways in the speedboat. I was hungry most of the time. Every day we had ramen noodles for breakfast, and then only cookies or some other snack until our supper of rice and fish. Nights were even more difficult. Mosquitos were rampant most places, floors were hard, and noise was incessant. The election campaigns involved rock bands entertaining in many of the villages; in others, our hosts would rise before dawn and awaken us pounding chilies, cleaning fish or---in the wealthier settings---butchering chickens.

Our expectations about our living conditions had see-sawed dramatically since we first heard of the project. For months, I had assumed, based on my earlier experience in East Kalimantan, that our living conditions would be very primitive and physically difficult. Then we were called to the November meeting near Jakarta the year before---falling on Thanksgiving (we should have taken this as a bad omen!)---where we were told that the project would have radios, generators, refrigerators, a house for us near the Field Center, even possibly an airstrip put in for emergency use if we got sick. My image of life at DSWR changed. It is rarely hard to shift one's expectations of living conditions upward. As things turned out, I would have been better off to stick with my initial expectations!

We also found the conduct of the trip a bit confusing. Although Dudley was Chief of Party, Wim was our project officer, and he had worked in the area several years before. We expected him to take the lead during this initial phase. But we were never sure what the plan was on any given day; whatever plan there was seemed to change without warning; and we never seemed to get off early enough in the morning to avoid the intense heat of mid-day. We wondered if Wim might be expecting us to take more initiative, yet that didn't seem to make sense, given his own experience. We put it down to inter-cultural differences in expectations. He was Dutch, we were American.

We were also a bit baffled by their system of accounting for project expenses. We couldn't figure it out. How, for instance, could they give people perdiem and also pay for their food?

Back in Pontianak, exhausted, but enthusiastic, Wim, Enis, Dudley and I began work on our "Inception Report"---a more specific plan of action for the project, now that we had seen where we would work. When Wim and Enis had to leave in early June, Wim impressed on us the urgency of finishing the document within a few days, including an elaborate two year budget which needed to be approved right away. We continued working, again through the weekend, to get it done quickly. Wim left us with the promise to follow up with Jives on the equipment and vehicle purchases. We all agreed we would need them before moving upriver in August.

While in Pontianak, we had to make more visits to government offices to introduce ourselves and explain the project. Pak Toto again accompanied us on many of these visits. In one such meeting, he again showed his merit in an action that probably meant the difference between successfully building a Field Center and failing utterly. One of his superiors in a sister agency heard that we were building a Field Center. As we talked, it dawned on him that this meant a building....that government buildings have to meet certain specifications---specifications that, besides lengthening the time and money required to complete construction, also add at least 40% to the cost for a government-imposed tax.

Pak Toto could see the wheels turning in the other official's mind, and he predicted the direction of the conversation. He quickly said, "O, this isn't a real building. This is just a field post." He successfully diverted the official's attention to other matters, and we were able to proceed as planned.

'Alan's tutor was going home in early June, and she agreed to take him back to his grandparents' house in the US. Only a few days later we would have to make a return trip upriver. 'Alan would not enjoy the meetings and the endless hours in a speedboat that we knew lay ahead.

A Little More Reconnoitering

We needed to order our boats and make arrangements for a contractor to begin building the Field Center before we too went to the US for the month of July. TLI had wanted us to begin immediately in May, but we needed to see our other children in the US. We had negotiated the early starting date with the agreement that we would take a month of leave without pay in July. Our hope was that if we could get things going on this quick trip, significant progress could be made while we were gone. We knew this was an optimistic idea, but...we would try our best.

To our delight, our other son Brian called before we left Pontianak, saying he planned to come and visit us. He was in Europe on a special course and had a free week. Dudley went off to meet him in Singapore, while I headed back upriver.

Setting off by bus from Pontianak, I couldn't believe my luck. I would have some time to work (nearly) alone. No more group-grope travel. No need to worry about someone else on my team blowing the rapport I was carefully cultivating. I could orchestrate my own information gathering, plan my own day's travel. Aaah what delight!

My itinerary was one that would become very familiar to us: Take the bus (later, a car) on a 9 hour ride from Pontianak to Sintang, spend the night in the Flamboyan, a hot and noisy hotel in Sintang, and board our (hopefully) waiting speedboat the next morning. Travel five or six hours up the Kapuas, have lunch at Semitau or Selimbau, and carry on for another hour or so into the Reserve.

I had not actually succeeded in leaving Pontianak completely alone. I was accompanied by Parto, a nice, young Conservation Agency official, as well as our speedboat driver, Markan. We arrived at Pulau Majang in the far northern part of the reserve, and settled in at Bu Juleha's proto-hotel. She had a two story home, with a small storefront downstairs, and a large room on which sleeping mats could be spread upstairs. With the exception of the *camat*'s home in Lanjak, it was the most comfortable lodgings north of the Kapuas.

Our first requirement was to visit the *camat* in Badau, the county seat, several hours up the Seriang River from Pulau Majang. Markan soon told me that the river was too low for our speedboat, we would have to go by canoe. We negotiated a fare to Badau which we thought quite expensive, knowing that people from Pulau Majang went there fairly regularly. We didn't quite realize, at that point, just how long the trip was going to take---thanks to the low water.

We left early in the morning, first passing along the edge of Lake Seriang, an area full of inundated bushes festooned in June with bright red flowers. It seemed like an outdoor Christmas, with reds and greens against the bright blue sky, all reflected again in the still waters. A few more minutes and we traveled through a green "tunnel" made of bushes overhead, reflected yet again in the water. Not long after that, we entered a narrow, fast-moving river, which we were to follow for nearly five hours.

Our driver was a shifty-eyed fellow, who we gradually realized was somewhat deficient in intelligence. Fortunately he came accompanied by his bright ten year old son. Our view of the lovely and varied forest flowers and overhanging leaves was only slightly obstructed by the son's tiny form, kneeling or squatting in the bow of the motor-driven canoe. As we negotiated the curving river, the son would shout out a warning to his father whenever floating logs or stumps lay in our path: "*Kayu*," (wood) he would yell, and then turn to make sure his dimwitted father had made the necessary alteration in course. We stopped now and then so I could photograph some flowers or the child could pick some fruit. Birds of striking colors could be seen in the tree tops or flying overhead; squirrels jumped from tree to tree. It was magical.

Our stay in Badau was less so. We had a long, hot, dusty walk to and from the *camat*'s office---and of course, he, like the other *camat*s, was away campaigning. On our way back to our canoe, we were stopped and beckoned peremptorily to the office of the border police. There they demanded to see our papers, only becoming civil after seeing our many documents. And then we had another five hour trip home, sitting up unsupported in a tippy canoe. I remembered a thought that had frequently passed through my mind as I daydreamed about pleasant experiences on Borneo waters---that "I could happily spend my lifetime on a river in Borneo." Beware idle wishes! I began to wonder if maybe I wasn't getting too old for these adventures, as the ache in my back got worse by the hour.

That evening while I was relaxing in Bu Juleha's "hotel," her brother, Agus, came in with a female Proboscis monkey. These creatures are common enough within the Reserve but are on the endangered species list globally. Agus sat down near me and began to feed cassava to this little creature. She was extremely cute, with a pert little nose, and orange fur, and it wasn't long before the reason for his visit emerged: He wanted me to buy her. I made the first stab at what would prove to be a frequent spiel. I explained first that we were in a wildlife reserve---which in itself was news to most people, including Agus---and that the animals in a wildlife reserve had to be free. The idea that they should be free was also alien. It would be impossible for me, I said, to buy an animal, even if I were so inclined, because it was strictly forbidden by the Indonesian government---but that of course we wouldn't be "turning people in" for violations of this law now, since so few people knew about it. Agus left me with a curious expression on his face, shaking his head over these strange notions.

After our official trip to Badau, Parto headed back to Pontianak; and I was free to begin doing some research. I had a few days to study the local Melayu dialect, map the village, note down community facilities, learn a little about local fishing practices, and get to know some of my future neighbors. This was what I had come to Borneo for, this was what made the heat, the mosquitoes, the boring food, worthwhile. Learning about people is infinitely fascinating to me, and worth almost any physical discomfort. I was happy, truly happy.

Pulau Majang had its physical delights as well. It borders on Lake Seriang, and whenever I felt like it, I could go out on the dock and take a swim in the black water---now much cooler than what we had experienced in Lake Luar only a few weeks earlier. At dusk, the sunset was a feast for the eyes. Sometimes it would cast a lovely light on the green hillside of Bukit Empaik across the lake. Other times lovely pinks and purples would streak the sky, a beauty doubled by reflection in the water.

I could stay at Bu Juleha's house, which had a second floor with room to hang my mosquito net. When I came alone, she lent me a mattress---a true luxury! And Bu Juleha could cook! For the first time, I was able to eat regularly, even occasionally getting a cucumber or some cassava leaves to augment the monotony of fish and rice. She even had indoor toilet facilities, and occasional electricity and cold drinks!

By the time I left Pulau Majang, to meet my husband and son, Brian, I had had a little satisfaction and was quite happy to see them. Markan took me down to our planned rendezvous point, the Istana Kapuas ("Kapuas Palace"), which we had decided to use as our temporary headquarters and residence. It was without a doubt the most luxurious accommodation in the Lakes area.

The Istana Kapuas was a brand new floating hotel, with three tiny rooms, moored to the banks of the Kapuas in the village of Selimbau.

Two of the rooms were about 8' by 5', and the third was much bigger...maybe 8' by 10'. Each room had one bed with a cotton mattress and a bare light bulb (which operated when the generator was running). When a guest arrived, an overworked young woman would bring one sheet two inches larger than the top surface of the mattress, a long cylindrical pillow called a "Dutch wife" (a leftover from Indonesia's colonial history), and a regular pillow.

Air (and mosquitos) circulated through the room via the louvered glass windows and the air spaces under the roof. We learned that the establishment also provided *obat nyamuk* ("mosquito medicine")---an evil looking green coil which burned thru the night and significantly reduced the mosquito population. We always wondered what it might be doing to our lungs, but its effectiveness against mosquitos reduced our other concerns to inconsequentia.

The three bathroom stalls were large and clean. A periodic concern of ours was that these facilities were located just upriver from our rooms and the kitchen. The location of the kitchen beneath our room meant enforced early rising. The blaring of music late at night on the prized sound system constituted a potent reminder to all that Selimbau had joined the modern world and an effective impediment to needed sleep. My husband sometimes theorized that the secret to Third World "underdevelopment" might be very simple...lack of sleep.

The owner of the Istana Kapuas, Telly, was a fascinating character. He was in his early thirties, the bright son of a Pakistani man and a Melayu woman. He had lived for about ten years in Jakarta, modeling of all things, but decided after he married there, to come back to his home town with his new skills and sophistication, and try to improve things for himself and his people. Besides the Istana Kapuas, he owned a couple of *motor*s and co-owned a private religious school in Selimbau.

We were very lucky to meet Telly and put our trust in him, because without his help I doubt if we could have succeeded in getting the Field Center started when we did. The British Government, which was funding the project, needed three formal bids on the costs of Field Center construction. Telly found us three carpenter/contractors willing to bid on the project. One of them we quickly realized was the obvious choice: Haji Idui.

The Invasion of Bukit Tekenang

Telly was as interested in us as we were in him, and we had long talks---especially during his nightly vigils adjusting his electrical system so that the fluorescent bulbs would stop flickering incessantly. We learned from him that he had been chastised for failing to report our presence to the local police during our previous visit. We realized that we would have to talk with them anyway, so we set out on the rather long, hot walk to Selimbau's compound of government buildings.

Along the road, we were followed by hordes of children, and called to continually---a common experience in Indonesia but one that my husband finds particularly annoying. I berated him mildly for refusing to respond pleasantly to a woman who invited us home with her. He gave me a sardonic look and said, "Yes, I guess if you saw an orangutan walking down the street, you'd want to take it home and show your friends too." I knew the feeling!

On our way to the police station, which we considered our destination, we went by the *camat*'s office. Younger officials came running out of that office, beckoning to us and inviting us in. No, we explained, we just wanted to report to the police.

Nothing is ever as simple in Indonesia as it should be. Once in the police station, about ten police emerged, all apparently intent on keeping us there as long as possible. No sooner had we shown one person our multitudinous papers (permission letters, agreements between governments, passports, copies of passports, photos, etc., etc.) than someone higher up appeared who also wanted to peruse them all.

When we finally escaped from the police station, the officials from the *camat*'s office came out and ushered us inside, insisting that Pak Ali, the *camat*'s representative (the *camat* was out of town again), had to see us. We were getting a bit disgruntled, since we had a lot of work left to do and very little time.

I thought my husband might go apoplectic when he actually understood what Pak Ali had in mind. Pak Ali had learned from the rumor mill that we were about to return to Bukit Tekenang to select the exact location for the Field Center. He wanted to make an outing of this reconnaissance trip. Not only that, he wanted to bring along all the higher-ups in Selimbau, to spend the night there.

Dudley and I were torn between bursting out laughing or going through the roof. The raft homes of Bukit Tekenang had almost sunk when our small party of six had come to visit for half an hour the previous month. We wondered what on earth this man had in his mind. We could only assume that he'd never been into the Lakes area. With great personal restraint, we managed to acquiesce---we really did need the good will of local government. But we were not happy at the thought of starting our relationship with the inhabitants of Bukit Tekenang by being so closely associated with the Government, let alone possibly sinking their homes!

We returned to the Istana Kapuas, and gradually gained an understanding that Selimbau was basically run by a troika: The police, the military and the *kecamatan* personnel. At least three members of each organization would accompany us, plus the contractor and his helper. We owned one speedboat and one *longbot*; and one other speedboat was found---so long as we would pay the cost of the gasoline. We bought rice and vegetables and sugar and whatever else we thought the group might eat, as a good will gesture to the people whose homes we would be invading for the night.

Brian and I volunteered to ride in the *longbot* (which would take twice as long), again as a gesture of goodwill. We got off fairly early that morning and set off up the Kapuas to Nyibung, where we turned North into the Lakes area. We crossed Lake Bekuan and followed the Belitung River up past Sekolat (one of the larger villages in the Reserve) and through Lake Belida' to Bukit Tekenang.

We'd both had our fill of scenery that morning, so we used the time to catch up on his previous year at West Point. As I listened to his minor escapades and embarrassments and delights, I realized what a nice young man he'd turned into. During the first years I'd known him (he was really Dudley's son), I'd worried that he was too intellectual and reserved, that he couldn't unwind; and when he decided to go to West Point, that concern intensified. But I needn't have worried. He was a wonderful person!

At Bukit Tekenang, we found our colleagues assembled on one of the rafts, waiting for us. Brian, who was the least used to this aquatic environment, was the first out of our *longbot* onto a raft. We looked toward the shore, trying to find which log would provide the most secure footing. One route seemed best, and Brian started across it. He was perhaps halfway along the log when it began to roll. He made a very amusing sight, flailing his arms wildly, trying to get his balance, and finally falling---splash---into the water. The assembled group burst into uproarious laughter.

Although I recognized the humor, I felt a real twinge. How would Brian cope with this? What a relief when I saw his smiling face emerge from the water! He was laughing as hard as the rest of us. Our uptight youngster had turned into a self confident young man...with the valuable ability to laugh at himself. I couldn't really claim the credit, but I was still proud of him!

The rest of us opted to go by canoe. We wandered around Bukit Tekenang, wading through the thick ferns, looking for a place big enough for our Field Center. We knew we would need access to water---both for transportation and for domestic uses. We didn't want to disturb too many crops or raze too much forest. We hoped for comparatively flat land, and---in the best of all possible worlds---a nice view. Within an hour, we had selected a site, and were ready to accept the local folks' hospitality.

We all trudged onto one of the raft homes (with me praying all the while that it wouldn't sink), and sat on the floor all around the walls. We met Mat Tahar who was introduced, to our surprise, as the man who owned the land we would be building on. Women who were later to become dear friends served us what we quickly (and fortunately) realized was a local product and a regional delicacy, *salai*. We could see the pride and anticipation written on their faces as they passed us plate after plate of these smoked whole fishes---and watched for our reaction. We made a valiant effort to express an enthusiasm we unfortunately did not feel. I'm not sure whether we succeeded or not.

I remembered the importance of eating together as a way of bonding. I hoped that this might be some kind of a ritual of commensality, and a happy beginning for what would be a long and productive affiliation. I basked in the warmth I already felt toward these people. Such pleasant thoughts were interrupted by Pak Ali's preparations to depart. I quietly inquired whether he didn't plan to spend the night, and discovered that he had (wisely) changed his mind. We would be returning to the comparative luxury of the Istana Kapuas after all.

Land in Dispute

We returned to Selimbau, where we attacked the remaining tasks: Explaining what we wanted in a Field Center to Haji Idui and learning what he would need to accomplish the task. Three days before we had to leave Selimbau, we learned that the "governing troika" had called a meeting at the Istana Kapuas. We assumed it was to be a sort of finalization of all we were planning to do.

At the appointed hour, a variety of men in uniforms began arriving. More and more boats of varying sizes and shapes came, bringing more and more folks---including one particularly unpleasant looking fellow wearing the cap of a Haji (one who has made the pilgrimage to Mecca). I realized that I was the only woman in the group.

People were just about settled when the unpleasant looking Haji abruptly and forcefully began talking. "You can't have this land. The Germans came wanting it last year and the French tried to get it from us before that. You can't have it!" This short and rather explosive speech was a double whammy. First, all indications to date had been that things were going smoothly with regard to the land acquisition question (which we had worried about privately). Second, Indonesians very rarely indulge in aggressive outbursts of this kind. I realized that the onus of communication in this matter was going to fall on me as the more fluent Indonesian speaker.

I also found myself in a difficult ethical position. For years I had been defending local people's rights to traditional lands in Borneo---particularly against timber companies. And I expected, on this project, to be working with local communities to develop ways to allow local people to continue residing in the wildlife reserve. Although this was contrary to existing Indonesian law, the project had an implicit mandate to seek solutions to this real and ubiquitous problem. But now, before we could even start the project, I was going to have to play the heavy. I didn't like it at all....but I couldn't see any way out of it---particularly given the time constraints we were under.

I explained gently that we had asked the people at Bukit Tekenang and in the *camat*'s office, and been assured that the people there did not own the land. "In fact," I said, "since this area was a national wildlife reserve, even the *kecamatan*'s claim to the land was questionable. In Jakarta people argued that it belonged to the national government."

I knew I was in muddy waters. Land tenure laws in Indonesia are perhaps more disputed, contradictory, and ambiguous than any other legal matters. "Traditional laws" of land tenure apply, the provincial government has recognized claims, and the national government in some sense supersedes all else. Each dispute is actually handled individually.

The Haji continued the attack, I tried to counter, he would attack again, and again I would counter. I was debating something of critical importance in a dialect of Indonesian with which I was not yet familiar. I knew I had to maintain my cool. Getting angry is almost never effective in Indonesia. It certainly wasn't an option in this setting, though the man was infuriating. The effort was beginning to wear.

After quite some time, the Police Chief began to speak. I held my breath, petrified that he would bring all his authority down on this objectionable man. Though convenient in this particular dispute, it would have been a very bad sign for the project's long-term success. What a relief when he simply took the role of rational moderator. To my extreme surprise, he showed a great deal of sensitivity to local interests. In my earlier experience, in eastern Borneo, I'd found government officials to be singularly unsympathetic to the concerns of local people. The men of Selimbau's Troika were showing rationality and concern, and they were making sincere efforts to solve the problem to everyone's satisfaction. I was very surprised and pleased. This would bode well for future efforts to secure people's rights to land within the Reserve.

Our meeting ended without resolution---except that we would have to make one last emergency trip to Putussibau to get support from the *kabupaten* (District) officials in this matter. This trip---with only the three of us and Markan---went much faster, and we were able to get the support we needed. When we returned to Selimbau, the Haji's complaints had evaporated and he was in fact in Pontianak expressing his support for our project at the Conservation Agency.

The Beginnings of a Field Center

Our agreement with Haji Idui---referred to privately as "the good Haji"---was whittled out over the course of this incredible week. We had some rough sketches of what we wanted for a Field Center, but many critical details were missing. Over the course of the construction, the bulk of which took about six months, we realized again and again how lucky we were to have found such an honest and well intentioned contractor.

We finally sat down one afternoon in the incongruous green stuffed chairs of Haji Idui's living room, drinking Milo served by his wife. I jotted down several paragraphs outlining what he was agreeing to do, by what date, and what we were willing to pay him. We realized that the British Government was unlikely to be impressed with the hodgepodge of English and Indonesian hen scratches decorating my notebook. Did Haji Idui know where we could get a typewriter? Big smiles---Yes, he had one. Telly left and soon returned with an ancient typewriter, paper and carbon paper.

It was only when I put in two sheets of paper separated by carbon paper and began to type that I realized how important the carbon paper was. The typewriter had no ribbon. Our "original" was going to have to be a carbon! We just crossed our fingers and hoped that the British project's auditors would have a sense of humor. Once signed, we retired to the Istana Kapuas, where Telly treated us all to a meal of a very special and expensive local fish.

Once the Field Center seemed on its way, we had one more important task to accomplish. We had to design and order the two boats on which we would live. We had been making sketches of boat interiors for several days, whenever we had a momentary lull in our other activities. So on the last day we could possibly stay upriver and still make our plane reservations to the US, we bid Telly and Haji Idui a fond farewell, and made our way downriver to the home of Haji Walidat, Markan's patron in Suhaid. There we were assured that one boat could be ready for us in mid-August when we expected to return, and the other would follow soon after.

In the course of our boat-building discussions, we were invited to see a variety of Suhaid's pets. Word had gotten around that we were somehow connected with wildlife. There were snakes and lizards residing in aquaria, a purple heron tied to a raft, and---most dramatic of all---a very large and very long reticulated python. The man who owned the python brought him out along the public walkway, and let Brian and Dudley fondle it. I declined the honor. Bystanders said that it never bothered people and it would go home if told to by its owner---a trick my husband maintains we observed.

We returned to Pontianak barely in time to make our flights. But we were amazed that we had been able to do as much as we had, and wondered how much progress would really be made in our absence. We had had another two weeks with very little sleep, inadequate access to food, and some complex tasks which we had managed to complete in a very short time. We left for our month in the US, wondering when the pace was ever going to slacken. At least we'd been assured that the project's equipment would be waiting for us when we got back. That should make things a little easier.

The Bureaucratic Maze

After our visit in the US, we made the required stop in Jakarta on our way back to the field. Our project was run by TLI, which had a sub-contract with SCF, which in turn got project funds from the British Government, all somehow cooperating with the Indonesian Conservation Agency. It was very complicated. I hoped we would at least gain a better understanding of project financing from SCF. They might have neo-colonialist leanings, but surely they would be more sophisticated about project finance than TLI seemed to be.

Dudley, Wim, Jives and I agreed to meet one morning in early August. Jives, dressed impeccably as usual in a dark business suit and tie, was dripping good manners and sophistication. As he and Wim shook hands, I was again struck by the contrast in demeanour and attire. That these different personal styles reflected differing values and expectations re-surfaced immediately and very obviously.

We all talked about the weather, ate Scottish butter cookies, and drank tea, until I finally decided I needed to get some answers. Has the work plan and budget in our Inception Report been approved yet? Well, no... Was the equipment already on site? Well, no....In fact, the British Government was just then deciding on which company would be the purchasing agency. Would the equipment be there by the time we went to the field in mid or late August? Well, no....it would actually be about six more months until it got there. Could we buy the really important things now, and leave the less critical things for the purchasing agent? Well, no....we couldn't actually buy anything (other than the boats for which we'd somehow gotten special dispensation).

I finally turned to Jives--who had talked of building us a house, an airstrip, and all manner of unnecessary luxuries the previous November---and said, aghast, "But this means we won't even have any lights or any electricity to run our computers?" No response. "Do you realize that?" He looked at me without turning a hair, and said..."yes," without the slightest indication of personal concern or regret. This was an eye opener for me. When I had worked before in remote areas on complex projects involving many people, I had always felt the support people, back in "civilization" were concerned about me and my family. I was beginning to get the idea that maybe this would not be the case on this project.

The Boats

When, in late August, all official permissions had finally been acquired, we were ready to head once again upriver. Packing as much of our personal effects as we could fit into a speedboat, Dudley, 'Alan and I headed upriver, arriving at mid-day at Haji Walidat's dock in Suhaid, near the mouth of the Tawang River and the main entrance to the reserve. We spent the night of my 47th birthday on our first boat, the Buaya Biru I (Blue Crocodile I), under construction in Suhaid.

I felt a little sorry for myself: I had no cake or presents; I was hungry again; and my husband and son were both in ill humor. Dudley was struggling to fashion our electrical system before it got dark---with a 500 w portable generator that TLI had bought us from its own budget; and 'Alan was adjusting to the lack of fans and cold drinks, and to the monotonous diet of the Lakes area.

'Alan's general dismay was very brief. He soon took off to investigate his new surroundings, and within hours was back at the boat asking to spend the night with new-found friends. We gratefully agreed, knowing that he was just as safe in an Indonesian village as he was in his own bedroom. Next I saw of him, he was with a huge cadre of children, dressed only in their skivvies, sliding down the long muddy banks into the river---much as American children slide down snowy hillsides. His briefs were never quite the same.

Having lived on a sailboat in the US, and knowing my husband's penchant for privacy, I insisted that we needed two *motor*s, especially since they only cost a little over $1,000 each. We settled into the first of these peculiar 13 m boats, supervising the addition of shelves and other minor modifications.

As the Buaya Biru II neared completion, we were approached by the carpenter, Haji Walidat's son in law, for an advance to purchase some of the lumber he needed. We were surprised and asked if Haji Walidat had approved this; the son in law said he had, and we provided the advance. It turned out that Haji Walidat had found his far less competent son in law difficult to work with and had transferred responsibility for the second boat to him---much to our dismay. The Buaya Biru II was built with green lumber, which contracted over the first few months of habitation. For several months, strips of sunlight decorated the inside of our boat, streaming (like the rain) between the horizontal boards which formed our walls!

It was soon completed though, and we tied the two boats together, side by side. The finished products looked rather like small rectangular houses, each atop a hull. Although they are considerably more roomy (if less well designed for Westerners) than a normal, western-style, cruising sailboat, adjusting to life aboard was an ongoing trial.

Designed for shorter people, the Buaya Biru I (BBI) had a ceiling that was too low in the aft areas, even for me (let alone Dudley's 6' height). I cooked breakfast sitting down, bending over the stove, in a back-breaking position. Whenever we went out to the back of the boat, where the head and our access to water were located, we had to walk bent over, and perform whatever functions we chose to, stooped, squatting, or bent double at the waist. Any significant amount of time in that part of the boat (kitchen, bathroom, and access to 'Alan's canoe) resulted in severe 'lower back pain'. Even months later, when I made a special Valentine's Day meal of French bread, packaged soup, and fudge---a major feast for us---it took a half an hour in a horizontal position, moaning quietly from time to time, to recover from the sustained effort of cooking at a 90 degree angle.

Going from one boat to another posed special difficulties as well. The two boats did not sit exactly evenly in the water, so the entryways, which adorned the midsections of each boat, did not exactly match up. Bent double to pass through, we periodically caught our feet on the spring lines that kept the two boats properly positioned. On several occasions I narrowly escaped being pitched headfirst into the sitting room of Buaya Biru I.

Although some of these problems only became clear later, our first few days in Suhaid were spent solving the obvious difficulties for people our size in boats designed for those smaller and more agile. Once we had identified the crucial things to fix, we set to work to select a more permanent mooring place for our boats within the reserve. We were anxious to get to work.

Chapter III: Move Number One – To Nanga Pengembung

As soon as we could, we made a trip up the Tawang River to inspect the progress on the Field Center being built at Bukit Tekenang. We had arrived at the height of the dry season, so we were also constrained to keep to the big rivers. The lakes and small streams had all dried up.

So we were searching for our new home along the still navigable Tawang River. We were intrigued by the first community we came to, going downriver from Bukit Tekenang: The Melayu village of Nanga Pengembung.

Habiba and Mboi

Nanga Pengembung, like many Bornean communities, was at the confluence of two rivers. Indeed, *nanga* is the local term for a confluence. Coming ashore at that point, we found several boisterous boys and young men extracting some very big fish from their canoes, amidst much loud talking and laughter. One of the young boys took it on himself to answer our various questions about the fish, the gear, their fishing practices.

After a few minutes, we traversed the mud flats between the river's edge and the village proper. We climbed up a rickety ladder to an even more rickety boardwalk, high above the ground. The village of Nanga Pengembung stretched for roughly a city block along the Tawang River, the houses laid out on either side of the boardwalk. We walked slowly and cautiously, worrying all the while that our greater weight might be the final straw for a structure that looked about ready to collapse on its own! People chattered at us and welcomed us, very amused at the concentration we were devoting to what they considered the very simple act of walking. We rarely dared look up from the boards and poles that creaked and swayed and threatened to break beneath us.

Perhaps 2/3 of the way along this boardwalk we encountered an unusually friendly woman in her mid-30's. Habiba was outgoing, vivacious, pretty, and we were amazed to discover, mother of ten and grandmother of four. She took us in hand, and invited us to "her" house. Had we realized at the time that it was the last house on the boardwalk, we might have elected to get back into our boat, but...."ignorance is bliss," and we followed her charming lead.

We went with her to the largest house in the village, actually owned and occupied by her husband's nephew and his wife, with two young daughters. When we expressed our interest in possibly moving there, they took us back...along the same rickety boardwalk... to the head fisherman's home. This dignified, old, white haired man assured us that we would be most welcome in his community should we decide to come. We were so taken with the friendliness and hospitality of these people, that we more or less decided on the spot to move to Nanga Pengembung when our boats were ready.

A week or so later we brought the Buaya Biru I to Nanga Pengembung, and moored it toward the upriver end of the village, near Habiba's family---explicitly to avoid the village's sewage and other refuse. We soon discovered that Habiba and her family---her husband, daughter, son in law, and two younger children---actually lived in a small hut beyond the boardwalk. They, as well as the family in the big house, used the raft to which we tied our boat, so we quickly gained an unusual intimacy with the whole family.

We watched Habiba and her 14 year old daughter, Mboi, wash their food, dishes, clothes, and bodies, just outside our door several times a day. We saw Edi, Mboi's young husband, standing on the boardwalk, watching the women work day after day. The whole family brought their fish catches to the raft to clean, making an impromptu party at which we were happily accepted. 'Alan and Habiba's son, Beli, became fast friends. Habiba, we learned was a *dukun*, or traditional healer. I found her to be the most congenial woman in the community. She had experience in city living, and although I could see she was flattered that I liked her, she also felt fairly comfortable with me. We became friends.

One day in October, after we'd settled in fairly nicely, we heard a commotion outside. A voice that we soon recognized as Habiba's was raised in anger, a rare occurrence in Indonesian villages. Although we couldn't understand everything she was saying (her language was Melayu), we got the general gist. She was screaming at her son in law, berating him for his unreasonable jealousy and for his unwillingness to leave Mboi---even briefly---to go do his own work. She accused him of following Mboi around, not even letting her eliminate her bodily wastes without him. We too had noticed that he spent inordinate amounts of time watching or accompanying his pretty and very young wife.

Habiba's dramatic and loud diatribe continued for nearly an hour, with much repetition, posturing and slamming of pans and other household goods. No word was heard from Edi. Not long after things quietened down, she emerged on the raft. I welcomed her, secretly dying of curiosity and hoping against hope that she would explain her outburst. There is of course no privacy in this kind of environment. Although mildly embarrassed, she explained that she had been at her wits' end. Edi did nothing to contribute to family subsistence, and drove her daughter crazy with his completely unfounded jealousy. She had spoken to him about it repeatedly in private, with no effect. In the end she had done this to shame him into changing his ways.

Mboi is a lovely little thing, whom I had worried over, sad that she had married so terribly young (at 13, like her mother before her). I asked her once if she had wanted to marry Edi. She answered shyly, "I just received whoever wanted me. I didn't choose." I had the definite impression that this was what young girls are supposed to say. Neighbors said her parents had pushed the marriage. The parents maintained that Edi had been so persistent and so frantic to marry her that they'd finally agreed. But all agreed that the marriage was not going well.

Not long after this, I heard strange sounds, like sobs, groans, even something like a scream, nearby. As I left the boat to investigate, I saw a cluster of people carrying a wriggling body up the steep ladder into the large house on the boardwalk. I went up to see what was going on. We kept medications, not otherwise available, on the boat, and I thought they might be needed. Although frequently confronted with medical problems and emergencies, they still frighten me.

When I got there Mboi was thrashing about uncontrollably on the floor. I was pretty sure she was having a major epileptic seizure. I could feel the room begin to spin, realizing there was nothing I could do, remembering when my own daughter had a much less dramatic seizure 15 years earlier and how terribly frightened I had been then. That incapacitating fear came back to me clearly. Here was my newfound friend, and her lovely daughter, struggling with a much more dramatic version of the same problem, without any possibility of the professional diagnosis or access to treatment that I had had.

Breathing deeply, I managed to pull myself together, and as soon as the seizure passed, I got some history. Mboi had a very high fever a year or so earlier, and since that time had been afflicted with this problem several times. She seemed otherwise normal, but when she suffered from some stress, she might have a seizure. There is no possibility that her family could afford the daily dose of medication that could probably control the seizures---even if it were available. And epileptics don't live long in an environment where they are very likely to fall into the water and drown if they don't happen to have a seizure in the house.

Later I squatted on our raft with Habiba and Mboi. Habiba, worried sick about her daughter, also complained about how difficult Mboi's illness was on her, how tired it made her, and how much watching Mboi added to her already full workload. I felt sorry for Habiba, but even more so for Mboi who listened to her mother's complaints, her own emotions carefully hidden. Mboi could not alter her condition.

Shortly after Mboi had recovered somewhat, she took a bushknife, went into the forest, and tried to kill herself before some young men disarmed her. When she came back, she refused to sleep with her husband. The elders gathered on a subsequent evening to try to persuade the young couple to try again to make their marriage work, which Mboi and Edi agreed to do. But several months later the husband was gone, and Mboi, reputed to be pregnant, had gone to Pontianak to stay with some of her brothers and sisters.

DSWR Wildlife

My husband, who had worked in protected areas in Africa, was rather disillusioned with the paucity of obvious wildlife in the reserve. From the beginning, we were on the lookout for whatever we could find. On one of our first few days, Guntam (Habiba's nephew) came home with a nearly dead hornbill. It had apparently gotten caught in a gillnet and nearly drowned. It did not last long. As we toured the reserve over the months, we regularly saw captive Purple Herons (*Ardea purpurea*). These birds are magnificent in flight, but make a sorry spectacle, tied to rafts, fluttering their wings in fear whenever people approach.

A short while after we'd settled in in Ng. Pengembung, TLI sent us a poster showing the wildlife common in another wetlands reserve in Borneo. I decided one evening to check these species out with our wise old headman. I knew I could find him, relaxing on his veranda overlooking the river at dusk, enjoying the view; and I looked forward to talking to him again. He was always terribly busy, so a sustained conversation with him would be a rare treat. The poster excited his interest---and that of everyone else in the vicinity. They all started naming off the species---turtles, dragon fish, otters, pythons, hornbills, kites, crocodiles, etc. My pen was writing at full speed. I needed all these local names!

We began discussing conservation of endangered species. They seemed to understand and approve of the general idea of protecting species that were in danger of extinction. They freely discussed the dragon fish, or *Arwana* (*Scleropages formosus*)---a fish which the Chinese believe brings good luck. Traders have sometimes paid thousands of dollars for a single fish, resulting in a number of boom years in DSWR. Most of the best houses in the area are said to have been paid for by the lucky catch of an *Arwana* during those times. Prior to the boom, people simply ate them. The fish is almost gone from the wild, though they are now raised in fish farms in Pontianak.

The headman and his friends told me that persuading fisherfolk to protect some species--notably otters, turtles, and crocodiles---would be almost impossible. These creatures continually damaged fishing gear, and competed for the same fish the people ate and sold. The assembled group made it quite clear that they hated otters, particularly; turtle meat got a very good price when sold in Malaysia---though they, as good Muslims, wouldn't dream of eating it; and crocodile skins were very valuable, though they all agreed there were very few crocodiles left. By the time I left, I had a nice introduction both to the common local species and to people's attitudes toward them.

A few days later, Pak Abdulatif, who lived in a raft home moored right downriver from our boat, called to me. He had accidentally caught a beautiful water lizard of some kind while fishing. This black lizard's body was perhaps a foot long, with golden polka dots all over it. As we would do so many times over the next year, I bemoaned the fact that we had no books for identifying animals or plants!

Pak Abdulatif then proceeded to use the lizard as a living model as he fashioned a simple trap---I had been inquiring about the various kinds of traps used by local people and he knew I'd be interested. There was a lively discussion, later, of whether or not this lizard's bite was poisonous. Pak Abdulatif had not let it bite him, but he had held it with no apparent fear; yet the headman argued that his brother had died not long after being bitten by one.

'Alan Injures his Leg

Even before moving to DSWR, I was plagued with a new and strange sense of impending doom---not about the project, but about our private lives. As our arrival date approached, and as we settled in, the fear increased, particularly about my son. I imagined he would fall from the boardwalks and break something, that he would be bitten by a poisonous snake or a crocodile, that he would hit his head falling off a raft and drown. I also imagined that Dudley or I would have a heart attack or some other medical emergency. I puzzled over these uncharacteristic concerns. I was used to meeting new situations with a certain degree of equanimity.

Soon after we arrived in Ng. Pengembung, 'Alan indeed fell. Balancing on a plank en route to a raft, he was pulled into the water when his cast net caught on a snag. He had what looked like a nasty bruise---along with a bruised ego, because the man with whom he'd been fishing laughed at his tears. Dudley left on a trip to Pontianak, and 'Alan's bruise turned into a festering sore. In a few days, his whole leg had swelled up, like a balloon, he came down with a raging fever, and eventually couldn't even walk. We had the worst night I ever hope to have with him. He lay in Dudley's place on our mattresses, and I sponged him off with cool rags and alcohol, trying to make him more comfortable. He is normally rather oblivious to pain, so his occasional low moan pierced my heart. I knew he was hurting, and I kept wondering how I would ever forgive myself if he died in this remote place where I had brought him.

I put him on antibiotics, and decided I had to take him to the doctor in Suhaid---but our speedboat had not yet returned from the trip to Sintang, with Dudley. I made 'Alan as comfortable as possible in a longboat, and hired someone to take us to the doctor. When we got to Suhaid, two hours later, we discovered that the clinic was at the top of what, at the height of the dry season, had become an imposing cliff---and my 100 pound son couldn't walk. The doctor refused to come down. Finally a slim young man in a nearby *bandung* kindly offered to carry him up the treacherous slope (including tippy planks, slippery mud, and rickety ladders!). I watched in fear and gratitude, as the man, roughly 'Alan's height but of wiry build, kindly scrambled up (and later, down) the cliff with my child on his back.

When we got to the doctor, he wanted to give 'Alan a penicillin shot (the standard solution for most ailments in Indonesia), and in retrospect, I suppose I should have let him. He argued that the oral Amoxicillin I'd given wasn't as good for this problem, but when I continued to resist he agreed that Amoxicillin would probably work. My new-found fearfulness was in full swing: I was afraid of dirty needles, and HIV/AIDS, and I still had a lingering fear that 'Alan might be allergic to penicillin. The doctor's recommendations differed from those in our book, *Where There is no Doctor*, and I, sadly, had more faith in the book than in Indonesian medical training. 'Alan was on medication for nearly two months, trying to keep his leg dry (a virtual impossibility in our riverine existence). His wound finally healed in November, leaving a nasty scar still visible on his shin.

Our New Tutor Arrives

In a few days my husband returned from Pontianak with 'Alan's new, 19 year old tutor and the news that my father would be operated on for stomach cancer during the next few days. The news came out of the blue. He'd been healthy last I'd heard...and this was a serious, life threatening disease. I struggled, over the next few weeks, realizing there was nothing I could do to help, yet full of internal turmoil, not even knowing if he were alive or dead after the operation.

Meanwhile, we had to try to help our tutor, Gillian, cope with the new environment. She had lived in Indonesia and Malaysia before, but never in such difficult conditions. Although we had planned together that she would live with a local family, none of us quite realized what that would entail.

She stayed with Guntam and his wife, Ayu, in the village's largest house. They were congenial and pleasant people, and we arranged for Ayu to cook for all four of us. Although in some ways convenient, it meant that we never had any privacy from each other either. Our boat was Gillian's only source of English, of common culture, of electricity----so she spent much of her free time with us.

At that time, we still only had one boat, of course; and our "living room" was about 2m by 2m. Evening would come, and 'Alan would retire to his room to read. Dudley and I would just be gearing up to sit quietly together and share our day, when a tall, lithe 19 year old girl would appear quietly in the doorway. Her expression showed her conflict. She didn't want to intrude. Yet no matter where she went, she was "odd man out." Not yet a part of the community, with no space to which to retreat, she could only come to us. And we could not really turn her away.

I have always thought of myself as more flexible than my husband, but this particular problem I found more difficult than he. I wanted to help her and make her feel at home; yet I also desperately wanted some time with my family. I could never really relax until she went home. It was a few weeks later---when I was almost at my own wits' end---that I discovered she was sharing one mosquito net with Guntam and Ayu's two little girls! She couldn't even sleep alone.

She was a remarkably adaptable young woman, but we all had some very difficult times to live through---adjusting to each other and to the new environment that confronted us. My father's ill health probably did not contribute to my ability to cope with such difficulties.

Sahar

Sahar had lived for seven years in this village of less than 200 people when I met him. About my age, with only a grade school education, he has an insatiable curiosity about the world. He watches television, the only regular source of world news, and reads whatever he can get his hands on (which of course is not much, in that environment). He knew all about the Earth Summit in Rio, and on his own, linked the arrival of our conservation project with the decisions made there.

He came to visit us on one of our first nights in Nanga Pengembung, and immediately engaged us in a substantive discussion of a recent decline in the local fishery, existing local fisheries regulations, and the failure of the government fisheries agencies to function effectively. Many of his observations about the environment and about the local community spoke of a genuine concern for the welfare of others and knowledge beyond what his formal education could have provided.

A few days later, he dropped by to let us know that if we were looking for anyone to work with us, he'd be interested. Noting his obvious intelligence, I soon took him up on his offer, putting him to work on some small studies I was doing in his community. Gradually, over the months, we used his services more and more. He always collected the data we were interested in, even going beyond it, coming up with ideas that would contribute to project goals. He seemed to want to work with us more for the intellectual challenge than for the money. Or perhaps he was simply convinced that what we were trying to do was of benefit to him and his community. In any case, he never mentioned money to us, accepting whatever we deemed reasonable.

This absence of greed became even more impressive as we realized how little money he actually had to support his family of six. He told me once that he'd counted up his family's expenses, and they needed to make about US$2 per day to break even (or a yearly income of $730). When he kept track of his income from all sources for us for several months, we found that he didn't make anywhere near that.

His wife, Amina, has borne him 6 children, two of whom died. When their youngest child, Hairani, was born, they were afraid he too would die. He seemed sickly. So consistent with local custom, they arranged for another family to adopt their baby. Hamiri and Timah paid a small amount of money for the baby, and are now called "father" and "mother" of Hairani---though Hairani remains in his natural parents' home. This custom is designed to trick bad spirits that might harm the baby; and Sahar and Amina are convinced it worked. Hairani was still thriving at two years of age.

Sahar's attempt to protect his child by magical means may seem peculiar, given his obvious intelligence, worldliness, and other traits we understand and value. But he lives in a setting where every week or so there is news of another death; and serious illness is a commonplace. In the few months we were in that community, the head fisherman's wife died; Pak Abdulatif's son had a fever so high he was repeatedly unconscious over a one month period, and later Pak Abdulatif himself was bedridden with fevers and chills for a month; a 4 year old child lost the use of one of her legs after a high fever, just before we came; and of course Mboi had epilepsy. There are undoubtedly other cases we don't know about. Sahar lives in a world without immunizations, without clean water, with only glimmerings of modern medical care. Magic is often the only recourse he has to protect his children from sickness and death.

Timah

Shortly after our arrival I noticed the presence of numerous tiny agricultural fields out behind the village. I had worked with agricultural scientists for years, and was interested to learn just how important agricultural produce was to these fisherfolk who lived in a wildlife reserve. My interest was piqued even further as I realized that agriculture was women's work here.

After a few meanders through the fields, I asked Sahar whom he considered to be the most knowledgeable farmer. He said Timah would be the best one to talk to, and he offered to accompany me and translate. I explained that I wanted to talk to her by myself because it was important for me to get the woman's point of view, that women were often shy to express themselves with men around. He felt she would be shy with me, because I was a foreigner and her Indonesian wasn't very good. I assured him I was happy to be patient with her bad Indonesian, and I would try to overcome her shyness. I needed to gain some fluency in Melayu anyway.

Feeling confident that Sahar understood, I headed downriver toward her house. I found her easily and explained what I wanted to do. She was a bit uneasy at first, but willingly came with me to the fields and began showing me who owned which plots. I explained that I wanted to measure the plots later. As we proceeded around the field, she began to unwind. Whereas at first she had answered my questions in monosyllables, she began giving fuller responses. She even began asking me questions. We were getting along very well and I was pleased. After we had gone all around the cluster of plots---and gotten very hot and sweaty---we found a shaded log on which to sit down and cool off, and I began to ask her some more focused questions. I really felt that we were beginning to click, when to my dismay, Sahar appeared out of the blue with two or three other men. They plopped down nearby, and began "helping" me---rephrasing her views, elaborating on them, translating them. She very quickly stopped talking.

I was tired and hot and aggravated since getting her to open up in the first place had been a somewhat difficult process. I was further irritated since I had already told Sahar that I didn't want him to "help" me with this, and why. I tried again to explain that I wanted to hear what she had to say, but they just repeated that she didn't know Indonesian very well. She clammed up completely. After trying several tacks unsuccessfully, I finally just stalked off in a frustrated huff. I could tell immediately by the amazed and fearful looks on all of their faces---and my own knowledge of some probably pan-Indonesian cultural norms---that I had made a bad mistake. My peculiar and persistent questions could easily be overlooked, but my ruffling of smooth social relations was harder to forgive.

There were already many bizarre rumors about our purposes in the region---some said we were there to blow up Bukit Tekenang or dig it up for gold or antiques, that we needed a pregnant 15 year old girl to bury under the posts of our Field Center, that we were looking for a legendary shrimp with diamond eyes, and so on. I'm sure these rumors, combined with my socially unacceptable outburst, convinced Timah that I was definitely *not* to be trusted.

I returned to our boat, pretty sure that I would be sorry for that outburst for a long time. Sure enough, she refused to go out to the fields with me anymore. I tried to regain her trust by choosing her as one of our daily recordkeepers (for which I was paying a small, but normally welcome, amount of money), but nothing worked. I had definitely blown it with her.

A Set-back

But all was not lost. The rest of the community was still cooperating, and I was making good progress. By early October I had completed a census, finished measuring the agricultural fields, begun a study of indigenous fish classification, and gotten ten families going on a recordkeeping study of their resource use. I was entering copious daily fieldnotes in my computer, and felt that things were going very well. I was mildly concerned that my computer's A-drive had quit working, so I couldn't make backups, but I was very grateful to have the computer to use. We were still waiting for all of the equipment which was to have been delivered first in May, then in June, then in....

With all the studies underway, I decided to take a few days, and enter some of this data. For years I had had a still unattained goal: To enter my data as I collected it, so that my team and I could use the results while the project was underway. Although the project had still not provided us with the computers they'd promised, I had foiled them. I had brought my own! And although we didn't have our counterparts or any assistants yet, heck, I could enter my own data! I certainly had before.

I sat at the computer, slaving away for several days in the boat's steamy sitting area, entering the census data. We didn't yet have room for a proper desk, so I sat on the floor, typing on a bench in our sitting area. The feeling in my back reminded me of my ten hours in the canoe on the trip to Badau.

I was interrupted at this task, one afternoon by a strange man, carrying a basket which was tied closed. He didn't speak much Indonesian, or at least seemed to have a lot of difficulty understanding me. By careful and patient questioning---eventually mostly directed at his son---I managed to learn that they had walked for several hours from the community of Genting, across the dry bed of Lake Pengembung. Inside their basket was a baby long-tailed macaque (*Macaca fascicularis*). It, like Pulau Majang's Proboscis, was extremely cute. It played and cavorted all over our tiny living area---messing with my papers, peeing on the floor, and generally wreaking minor havoc. It wasn't long before I realized the reason for their visit. Again, they wanted me to buy it---for Rp. 100,000. I gave my canned spiel again---"This is a reserve, and trading in animals is forbidden within the reserve."

Still the man and his son sat on. At first I tried to make conversation...the language barrier made it all rather awkward. Eventually I tried silence, thinking that might prompt them to go home. I really did want to get back to work. No such luck. After quite a long period of silence, they offered to sell me the monkey for Rp. 50,000. They thought my canned spiel was simply a tactic to get a lower price! They finally did go home, with something of the same perplexed expression on their faces as I'd seen on Agus' in Pulau Majang.

Gleeful after I'd entered all the census data, I did a few analyses: Sex ratios, number of children ever born to the women, birthplaces of inhabitants, residence status in Nanga Pengembung or elsewhere, etc. We would soon be writing a quarterly report, and I was sure these findings would really be interesting to future team members.

All three volunteers were expected to be coming within the next few months, though none had gotten their visas yet---a perennial problem in Indonesia. All were eager for information about their future DSWR home.

I took a lunch break and went back to my computer, to finish off the few remaining parts of the analysis. I turned it on, but it told me that there was no such drive. No such drive? I called my husband, much more of a computer whiz than me. What's wrong with this thing? He played with it for a few minutes. I could see that his news was not going to be good....the hard disk had died.

The data entry and analysis were tedious, but I could do them over again. But the notes were really irreplaceable. It was several months before we were completely sure that there was no reasonable way to get them back. In the end, they were simply lost---lost to the humidity, the heat, the moulds and fungus of the tropics.

Good News

In September we learned that we were soon to receive a visit from Hugh, the coordinator for the British volunteers with whom we were to work. Hugh would inspect our facilities and determine whether the conditions were suitable for their volunteers. We knew that this British program required a private room for each volunteer, and we were wondering how we could arrange that (especially given Gillian's experience).

Dudley had recently gone through some trial scenarios for occupancy of the six bedrooms in the Field Center---all of which indicated there would be less room than the folks from TLI and SCF expected. He had already mentally abandoned the promised "room to himself" in the Field Center---wryly remembering the SCF promises of the year before. We couldn't quite see how we would be able to fit the existing and anticipated personnel into only three empty rooms---as would be necessary if each volunteer had a room to him/herself. I was also concerned that they spend as much time as possible in communities, since we were trying to work collaboratively with local people.

Hugh was one of our first visitors, and we were relieved that he seemed able to adjust to the tight quarters and constant balancing act that constituted life in the reserve. We took him on a tour of the future Field Center, where we all "tight rope walked" across the beams which would eventually support a floor. The place was abustle with some 30 workmen, measuring, hammering, sawing, some perched high on the roof beams, others digging holes for the septic system.

Pak Wawan, the foreman, was a closet intellectual who welcomed our visits with obvious pleasure. We represented both an opportunity for him to display his amazingly wide range of interests as well as add to his store of knowledge. He knew something about Darwin, biology, conservation and various other topics which amazed us---to his obvious delight. He was also an excellent foreman.

On this occasion, Dudley noticed some workers hammering in screws. Fearing they might be doing it out of ignorance, he sought out Pak Wawan to investigate. "Why aren't they using a screwdriver on the screws?" Dudley asked. "Don't they know you shouldn't hammer screws?"

"O yes, of course you should use a screwdriver," said Pak Wawan, "but our screwdriver disappeared."

"Why don't they use another one?" Dudley asked.

"O, we only had one," responded Pak Wawan.

Thirty men, building a structure consisting essentially of three, full sized houses, managing with one screwdriver! Yes, this was Indonesia!

We took Hugh on to Sekolat and Ng. Leboyan, other possible locations where the volunteers might stay. On the trip, he filled us in on what was happening in Jakarta. We'd already learned, with considerable glee, that we'd be getting very experienced co-workers. One was a fisheries expert with some ten years of experience who planned to use this assignment partially to collect data for her Ph.D. The other volunteer also had years of experience; he'd been doing conservation education in remote areas of the Pacific. They sounded perfect!

Now Hugh explained that they'd be arriving any day in Indonesia, but would have two or three months of language training in Yogyakarta first. They had also not yet received clearance from the Indonesian Government, but this, Hugh explained, was normal. He was sure they'd eventually get the clearance. We recognized the utility of language training, but were a little disappointed that we still had another three months without access to their expertise and help. Maybe some of our promised Indonesian counterparts would materialize in the interim.

By the time Hugh left, he'd decided that conditions at DSWR were acceptable for the volunteers. Although he'd stressed his concerns about physical conditions, I was also sure that he was checking us out as well. I was relieved that we'd "passed the test." We really wanted those volunteers up there. He emphasized the importance of saving rooms for them at the Field Center so that they would have the option of a room to themselves if they felt they needed it. And he'd raise the issue of living in a village with them. We could play that one by ear.

Yahoooo!!!

Romantic Interludes

Although the idea of living on a boat in the middle of Borneo has a definite romantic air to it, the reality was often less so. Yet we did manage to find a way to insert a little romantic togetherness into our overworked days. We arrived in the dry season, when the rivers are brown with mud and comparatively polluted with human and other kinds of excrement. This set us immediately to the task of identifying the best---most hygienic---way to bathe. Bathing is of course a recurrent necessity throughout the day when one lives almost exactly on the equator in an area "blessed" with such a hot and humid climate.

We had moored our boats at the upriver end of the village on purpose, but this did not entirely solve the problem. Besides bathing, defecating, and washing their clothes in the immediate vicinity of our boat, people regularly cleaned fish there. It was just not an appetizing thought----jumping into we-knew-not-what, or pulling up unknown "wonders" in buckets to pour over ourselves.

We developed a delightful solution. Every afternoon we left about 4, motored a canoe upriver to a deserted area and took our baths there. 'Alan was usually busy with his friends, so we could have a cherished, daily period to ourselves. We would bring along soap, shampoo, a towel and a sarong for me. Dudley could follow local custom and strip to his underwear.

We would motor a ways up the Tawang River, past a couple of fishermen inspecting their long lines near the island between the rivers, Tong and Tong Besar. These fishermen had been the lucky winners of the lottery for these two prized fishing spots. We'd pass canoes of married couples, or a parent and a child, returning from checking their gillnets or their fish traps further afield, tired but still friendly.

There we would come to a strange landscape, reaching northward. The banks of the river were gently sloping, and alternately composed of soil dried and cracked by the sun, or covered by a kind of peach fuzz of greenery, or just plain mud. Disembarking at our chosen spot, we could feel the soft mud squishing up between our toes, and delight in the welcome coolness of the water flowing over our hot, sweaty bodies. A paddle thrust into the bank provided a handy "hitching post" for our canoe. The silence, the cool, the privacy were a balm to my troubled soul. We could have each other's undivided attention, with a high probability of being undisturbed. We'd loll and float and dive and swim, playing together or keeping our distance, depending on our moods. Remembering that crocodiles lived here too gave me a bit of titillation every time we ventured out into the deeper water---though I never saw one out of a cage.

Or we could turn right off the Tawang into Tong Besar---the entrance to the soon-to-be-Lake Pengembung. There we could paddle among increasingly deeply submerged aquatic plants, and peruse the shoreline for Proboscis monkeys. There was a Proboscis family that lived in the trees bordering the river, and sometimes we could hear the strange grunts and groans characteristic of the male Proboscis. It reminded me of a male sealion's call. On lucky days, we could watch the male and a female or juvenile sitting on logs and tree limbs for a few minutes before they saw us and calmly sauntered away. They didn't seem particularly frightened.

One day I was mad at Dudley about something---I don't even remember what---so we went off to one of these secluded places to talk it out. He was paddling and I was haranguing him as we came out of a narrow passageway between Tong and Pengembung Rivers. He stopped paddling, as I was railing away at him, and the canoe got caught in a current. We began slowly whirling around. I remember his bemused, and then amused, expression as he tried to listen attentively to my rather unpleasant words while the water and the trees and the plants that surrounded us passed in gentle circles, round and round, behind me.

We usually paddled home from these daily jaunts upriver, letting the current help carry us home. We'd paddle lazily along, enjoying the comparative silence, and looking for wildlife. The beautiful stork-billed kingfisher (*Pelargopsis capensis*), the largest kingfisher, was a common sight, zipping across the river in front of us, a brilliant, iridescent blue, flashing in the sun. On a number of occasions we floated past the swollen carcasses of large and very dead reticulated pythons.

We would sometimes come upon a band of perhaps 40 Long-Tailed Macaques, scavenging among the debris on the exposed land between the forest and the water, just upriver from the village. The macaques, like the Proboscis monkeys, were not particularly perturbed by our presence, and would only meander away if we seemed to be approaching them purposefully.

These private outings surrounded by things natural---water, trees, plants, reflections, animals---soothed us after our often emotionally trying and physically exhausting days. They kept us "together" through some of the difficult experiences, more than any other single thing we did.

The Rains Come

We lived on the banks of the Tawang River. The river was an integral part of life. To get ashore, we had to cross it. We bathed in it, washed our clothes in it, got drinking water from it, used it for a toilet. It was our scenery, when we looked out the window. Dudley's and my rare moments of privacy were found in quiet places along the river, in narrow channels, hidden by dense foliage. When I asked how to get someplace, the river was always a point of reference. North and South were irrelevant, what said something locally was "upriver" or "downriver." It provided our neighbors' livelihoods. It was the avenue for communications and trade.

I was used to rivers. My home was in Portland, Oregon, between the Willamette and Columbia rivers---Nanga Willamette, it would have been called in Borneo. I thought of the river as something familiar and somehow solid, around which I could hang other aspects of my new existence.

In mid-October, it rained a few days. People began to say that the fishing season was almost over, that soon the seasonal fisherfolk would be leaving, and Nanga Pengembung would not be *ramai* (or lively) again until the next dry season (next June or July). I was curious to see how much things really changed with the changing season.

I woke up a few days later, and went out back to our head. As I peered down into the water, I got this strange feeling of utter disorientation. The river, which in my experience had flowed from the dry lakebeds in the North to the Kapuas in the South, was now going the other way! Was I seeing things? Did someone move our boats to a different location in the water? No, we were in the same place, and the water was indeed going the other way.

My neighbors reassured me, saying that this happened regularly when the dry season ended. The mighty Kapuas filled to overflowing from rains further inland, and it spilled its overflow into our lakes area, reversing the flow of the Tawang and all the other streams that had been flowing into the Kapuas. This event, that I found so discombobulating, meant that the rivers were high enough for our boats to get to Pulau Majang. In my own mind, I decided that when the rivers change direction, it must be time to move on.

The First Move

A week or so earlier, we had managed to bring our lab boat, the Rancong Loncat (or "Jumping Proboscis Monkey"), up the Tawang River. It had been quite an experience. We had taken the advice of Haji Walidat in Suhaid and bought a new diesel engine. He had recommended one with the unlikely name of "Dondong 13." When we got to Pontianak, and found that we could get a "Dondong 15" for only a little more, we did so. It was newly installed when we took off from Suhaid headed upriver for Nanga Pengembung. We had gotten about two hours upriver---diesel engines drive *motor*s veeeeerry sloooooowly---when the engine made a loud bang and quit. On inspection, the pistons had somehow frozen in their casings, and the engine was completely useless. We had bought a Dondong 15 rather than a Dondong 13 as instructed, and we were never to hear the end of that.

This was a financial setback and an inconvenience since someone would have to go back to Pontianak and try to get a replacement. But it didn't significantly interfere with our trip. Markan and friend simply lashed the *longbot* we were towing to the side, and pushed the *motor* along with a 9 hp outboard---at almost the same speed we had been going!

Anyway, the trip from Nanga Pengembung to Pulau Majang was going to be a little more complex. We had to move three *motor*s, a *longbot*, two speedboats, and four canoes--not to mention 'Alan's would-be-commercial fishcage! By this time, we had managed to fix the engine in the lab boat. I wondered how on earth they were going to manage this; I knew I wouldn't be much help.

The three *motor*s had been lashed together attached to "our" raft in Nanga Pengembung. These were untied, rearranged so that the bows of all three were heading upriver (which now, remember, looked like downriver), and tied together again. My husband and I, who both have quite a bit of boating experience, were trying not to interfere with their system. We knew they were used to dealing with this odd assortment of boats. But my husband kept shuddering uncontrollably at the line they were using, the knots they were tying, their cavalier attitude toward safety considerations. We knew that these folk were used to having to make do---they hadn't yet realized, for instance, that the project could afford to buy sufficient good rope for lines. In fact, we never managed to get that concept across!

The Rancong Loncat was then moved from the outside to a position between Buaya Biru I and II. The longboat and one speedboat were lashed to the sides of each of these *motor*s; and the rest of the boats were towed behind. What a strange sight we made, slowly chugging north by northwest.

We sat on the foredeck, and looked at the scenery along the riverbanks. Markan pointed out areas in Lake Seriang that he and Wim had traversed on foot, walking for hours during the dry season to get to nearby Empaik. It was hard to imagine this large lake completely dry, like a football field.

Much to my relief, we made it to Pulau Majang without incident. We had decided that we would like to moor our boats out away from the village, for privacy's sake. Although we needed and wanted interaction with local folks, we also wanted some time for our family as a unit. We would have to use our canoes whenever we left home, but that seemed a small price to pay.

Markan had selected a spot to the east of the village, in a bushy area along the lake's edge not far from the mouth of the Majang River. There, Markan and the young man we'd hired for the day set to work, tying our various boats together and to appropriately spaced bushes. Once safely moored, we couldn't resist the temptation to dive into the clean blackwater---far enough from the village so that we felt it was hygienic---and go for our first swim from our new home.

Chapter IV: Move Number Two - to Pulau Majang

Pulau Majang was a Melayu community of some 700 people, located on the northwestern border of the Reserve, close to the Iban communities that surrounded the Reserve. I still felt it was important to work with both ethnic groups, since they had very different ways of using their environment. TLI, as a wetlands organization, was naturally more interested in the lowland areas. But I felt that resource use in the surrounding hills could have significant impacts in the lakes (and I knew ODA was concerned about this issue). I was also pretty sure that the Iban did a lot more hunting of wildlife---something we were anxious to manage carefully---than did the Melayu. Being situated in Pulau Majang would give us easy access to both groups. Having had some introduction to the Melayu way of life in Nanga Pengembung, I was ready for the Iban.

Pak Mu'in

I was really chomping at the bit to begin work in the nearby Iban village of Empaik. Besides my professional "need to know" about Iban resource use, I'd been curious about them for years. I wondered how similar the Iban and the Kenyah, another dayak group with whom I'd worked, would be. I knew that before beginning research in Empaik I would have to remind the Pulau Majang village head (who was also technically head of Empaik) of my plan to conduct research in that community, and seek his advice on how best to proceed. We had already made a brief visit there together in June.

I was not surprised, and only mildly dismayed, when he insisted on taking me there again. Although I liked the man, I knew he was terribly busy. It appeared to me that he never had a moment to himself. Even more important, I didn't relish being connected in the minds of the Iban with this Melayu village head, whom I suspected of sharing the common Melayu view that the Iban were uncivilized. I also suspected the Iban were aware of that view and resented his titular authority over them. On the other hand, he was a likable and intelligent guy. He let me know one day in late October that he was going that direction and would be happy for me to accompany him. Realizing the inevitable, I jumped at the chance.

He explained that we must make a side trip to Pulau Majang's community rubber project where some folks would be working on their plots. I was intrigued with this unexpected opportunity to see a new aspect of resource use among the Melayu, and he was delighted with my offer of transportation.

To get from Pulau Majang to the south side of Empaik Hill where the rubber garden was going in, Pak Mu'in and I had to cross Lake Seriang, perhaps a ten minute ride in our small motor-driven canoe. We then entered a flooded area of fairly short, bushy trees---indeed this area was an extension of the lake at the time (though bone dry during the dry season). Vast areas of the Wildlife Reserve were covered with this bushy kind of vegetation. Although I understood they were ecologically unique, I had secretly been rather disappointed to see so much of this scrubby tree habitat.

In my mind, they didn't hold a candle to the huge, majestic, buttressed trees of Borneo's lowland dipterocarp forests. I didn't think these shrubs would be much of a draw for tourists, one of the development possibilities we were considering for the area.

After crossing the lake, we continued for another 15 minutes or so through these bushy trees, meandering this way and that as aquatic paths opened up here and there. We passed several canoes, loaded to the gunwales with people, baskets, and farming equipment, headed the same direction. At some point we entered the Empaik Damun River, eventually reaching the rubber garden.

On our way there I quizzed Pak Mu'in. This rubber project was initiated by the County Extension Agent from Badau, the county seat. Thirty-one families had agreed to work together clearing a hilly area across Lake Seriang from Pulau Majang, on the southern slope of Empaik Hill---the area used agriculturally by the Melayu.

A fairly large area of this clearing was divided into long, rectangular plots, measured out lengthwise from the end of the path leading to the canoe "parking" area---ensuring that everyone had roughly the same distance to walk to their fields. Specific plots were to be allocated using a lottery system. The Horticulture Department had provided the community with over 6,000 seedlings, which were visible at the edge of the field.

Near the seedling bed, the extension agent had prepared a sample plot demonstrating preferred rubber management. Trees were to be spaced 3 m by 7 m apart. Each tree was to be planted 60 cm deep on flattened ground, and surrounded by a short fence (60 x 60 cm) made of tightly spaced stakes. Land between trees was to be weeded. The people were told to use TSP, Urea, and Kcl---fertilizers also given by the project.

While Pak Mu'in helped the people laying out the plots, other men used chainsaws to cut large logs into pieces, thus clearing paths among the plots. Still others were burning trees and shrubs which had been cut and left to dry. I took the opportunity to walk over the whole area. Parts of it were peat soil; none of it looked like particularly good land. Indeed I was told that they wouldn't be able to grow rice on it, only rubber.

As this was all explained to me, I felt sad. Once again the government was pushing local communities to adopt cropping patterns and other management practices that would impoverish, rather than enhance, local natural resources. A monocrop (rubber) was being promoted in a context where crop diversity makes much more sense. Already impoverished soils on sloping lands were being exposed, when they should be covered. Another forested area was being cleared with government encouragement, when we were trying with a different government agency to reduce forest clearing. Not to mention the fact that the future rubber plantation was within the Wildlife Reserve---legally and ecologically incompatible uses of the land.

As all these thoughts were percolating through my brain, the intelligent and motivated Pak Mu'in was apologizing to me, saying that his community was inexperienced in rubber cultivation, that they were probably making mistakes in laying out the plots, that some of the seedlings had died, that the paths were not yet up to snuff. He did his best to cooperate with the governmental plans, in motivating and involving his community. He is justifiably proud that he managed to bring 31 families---all of them poor---together twice a week for roughly 6 months to work on these fields. It is truly a monumental accomplishment---particularly considering that these people will recognize no direct profit for at least 8 years! I could not disappoint this good man by voicing my true feelings. It was too late for that here.

After a few hours, we left for Empaik. He took me first to the Melayu fields on the southern side of the hill. From there I could walk to Empaik. He had, to my relief, decided to work in his ricefield while I went on to the Iban community alone. When I returned, pleased with my reception there, I mentioned that I wanted to learn the way to the Iban community by water so I could pilot my own canoe there. He suggested that we go there right then and mark the way. I was once again reminded of what a kind-hearted man he was.

The Way to Empaik

To get to Empaik village we had to make much of the morning's trip through the shrubs in reverse. But these bushy flooded forests are like a maze. From a canoe, you can't see over them, and they blend together, one looking very like another. It is very easy to lose your way. Fearing that I would get lost when I tried to go to the village of Empaik on my own, Pak Mu'in was trying to teach me how to navigate from Pulau Majang to Empaik.

When we got back that day almost to Lake Seriang, he showed me a break in the bushes to the West which would lead me to the village of Empaik. He had collected several old papers and plastic bags, which he began tying to branches of trees at decision points along our watery path. I felt like Hansel and Gretel! He was very patient, asking me each time we stopped if I thought I could recognize this turnoff or that shortcut. Our path sometimes followed a river; other times we seemed to be taking off through a forest. Still other paths---straight lines through the trees---had been created and maintained by the people. In some cases the trees came together above forming a low canopy. This canopy was reflected in the still waters, forming a visual tunnel. I was concentrating so hard on trying to learn the cues in this confusing and alien environment that I hardly noticed when we left the bushy trees behind, and came into an area where the trees were much taller.

Our setting changed very quickly from the familiar bushes into a tall, dark, mysterious forest. Trees came together far above from both banks, creating the appearance of Gothic spires and archways. The twisted support roots, visible above the water, of other trees were formed in grotesque and convoluted shapes. The brilliant tropical sun was virtually blotted out by these tall trees, with glimmers and glints of light appearing briefly and disappearing again, as our canoe moved along the waterway, creating unpredictable and beautiful patterns of light on the leaves and on the water.

We were now following the Empaik River. Its still waters looked an inky black from the canoe. I could see our bow cutting through a peculiar film on the water, in some areas. A little further along, our wake kicked up clear, tea colored bubbles of blackwater. I thought how I would love to make this trip without the noise from our canoe's engine. I didn't voice this thought to Pak Mu'in. I knew he would consider this a very peculiar idea. Local people used the canoes for transportation and for fishing, and they had only recently begun to have access to motors. From their point of view, engines were a great and wonderful benefit in their lives. Certainly no one who could afford to use an engine would paddle! Dudley and I knew that if we decided to encourage tourism in this area, we would have to get across the alien idea that paddling a canoe was a form of recreation for many people.

Pak Mu'in could see that I was delighted with this unusual place, just as I could see that he was not. He seemed to feel uncomfortable among these tall trees, and I couldn't deny that they had a spooky quality---like being in a European cathedral. The slime on the water gave an eerie atmosphere to the place; there were snake-like vines hanging from the trees and epiphytes sprouting like strange growths further up their trunks. But I was enchanted, sitting in a canoe, shaded by these lovely trees, cooled by the canoe's movement, watching an occasional bird flitting through the trees, fully enjoying the place's eerie qualities.

The river followed a tortuous route, requiring Pak Mu'in to exercise great skill in making the turns. The curves were so sharp that it would have been easy to get our bow stuck in one bank, and cram the engine into the opposite curve of the same bank. I remembered earlier canoe trips in East Kalimantan where I had, against a more experienced friend's advice, insisted on inexpertly wielding a paddle in the bow to keep our canoe on course. It had been exhilarating and slightly dangerous when the rivers were curvy and the waters were swift.

Although I thought I perceived some mild discomfort on Pak Mu'in's part, I hadn't paid much attention to it. Many, perhaps most, Melayu are afraid of both spirits and the Iban---either of which could have been the source of his feelings at this particular time. Before we had progressed very far beyond the bushy trees though, Pak Mu'in decided to turn back. Although we were now following a clear route along a riverbed, he decided that this was just "too complicated" a route for me to follow, that I simply wouldn't be able to do it, and he didn't want me to get lost; So we turned back.

But I had found a beautiful place to which I knew I would return.

Injan

Empaik is a village---actually a longhouse---of Iban Dayaks perhaps half an hour by canoe, and another half hour walking, from Pulau Majang. I wanted to learn about the Iban way of life and in what ways they used, benefited from, and affected their environment. But to do that properly I knew I would have to spend some time there, and learn their language. These Dayaks were very different from my Melayu neighbors.

By the end of October, I had been to Empaik several times and the people were becoming a bit used to me. So I decided to spend my first night there. I'd learned a great deal on the evening I arrived, walking all around the village area, visiting with many of the families in the longhouse, and taking short walks along a dirt road which had been made by employees of a nearby plantation-in-the-making.

One of the most disturbing bits of news was that a timber company had negotiated the people's agreement to log the beautiful forested area through which I'd passed with Pak Mu'in. In return, they were to get a small generator. Imagining the scene of their negotiations made my blood boil. Wealthy and sophisticated representatives of the timber industry persuading a community of illiterates that it would be in their best interests to trade what by all rights should have been their forests, for a generator worth a small part of one tree---and a generator they'd have a hard time getting fuel to run, to boot! It was also quite possible that this area was inside the wildlife reserve. Again I was reminded of our need to ascertain the exact boundaries of the reserve.

When I woke up the next morning, I decided to go investigate their agricultural fields. Meandering down a path I'd traversed before, I came upon a hut, with four women and a girl sitting in it, at the edge of a field. I recognized their faces from the village. There were two lovely young women in their mid-twenties (Bangkang and Caya) and a rather dumpy, stolid-looking woman of perhaps 30 (Mni'). I recognized the fourth as a feisty woman---also roughly 30---whom I had met and accompanied along this same path on an earlier visit (Injan). Bembang was Injan's daughter, an intelligent child of about ten. Recognizing Injan helped me overcome the shyness that always attacks me during the early stages of fieldwork---knowing the ambivalence with which rural people often confront strange newcomers.

As I approached them, I realized with surprise that the women were drinking *arak*, a potent alcoholic beverage. Although they welcomed me, I could see anxiety written on their faces. Injan, the woman I'd met before, fairly quickly launched into a statement (in a mixture of bad Indonesian and the closely related Iban language) of Iban customs. People should, she said, be good to other people. But if people did bad things to the Iban, their relatives would come and get even. I realized with a start that they were afraid of me! I quickly told them that my people also believed we should be good to others. The relief on their faces was obvious, though they were not yet fully reassured.

As we continued to try to talk to each other---their Indonesian was almost as bad as my Iban---they began to unwind. They told me that they were drinking *arak* because their husbands were among those who had left that morning for a moneymaking expedition to Malaysia. The men wouldn't be back for months, and the women would have to sleep alone and "cold" on their sleeping mats. They were drinking, they said, to forget their husbands' departure and to get warm another way.

They asked if I had any "medicine" to make (the to-my-eyes lovely) Bangkang fat like Mni' and Injan, to make her husband happy. I explained that I didn't, that Westerners always wanted to be thin, not fat; and they told me that was dangerous. If you were thin and got sick, you died more quickly. Mni' complained of a terrible toothache for which I promised to bring her some aspirin I had at the longhouse.

They offered me food which I "politely" refused. Their look of shock, and an outpouring of Iban that I couldn't understand, convinced me to retract my refusal and partake of their food. I later learned that for the Iban, touching the food is sufficient, but that refusing pointblank as I had done exposes one to magical dangers.

Injan launched into a glowing description of the pleasures of inebriation. She told of getting drunk, throwing up, and getting drunk again. She acted as though this was the greatest fun, doing graphic and hilarious imitations of upchucking. She made the most godawful, terrible faces for us, amidst considerable laughter, as she drank her *arak*. They all expressed their preference for *tuak* (a homemade rice liquor).

I recognized the same bluntness I'd been surprised at among the Kenyah, who would tell you how old you looked or how skinny you'd gotten, without a moment's hesitation. My new Iban friends told me about Bangkang's difficulty getting pregnant---saying that she wasn't "smart" at making babies. She had been trying to get pregnant for four years, yet they did not mince words, despite her sad face.

A young man came down the path hunting birds. Injan made a number of earthy remarks as he was approaching, including asking me if "I wanted him to use his big needle" on me. I was amused that they also referred to the same male body part as a "big gun." Since Indonesians often have rather overblown views of Westerners' sexuality, it seemed important to clarify early on that I was not looking for a man (He was also young enough to be my son!). I laughingly said I was only interested in my husband's, but I had the feeling they saw my response as a bit prudish, in our all-female context.

They had to get to work, and I asked if I could join them. They were surprised, amused, and readily agreed. Bangkang and Caya, the young women, sprayed the field with herbicide (without any protective face masks); and Mni', Injan, Bembang and I pulled weeds from around the rice plants. I had to have a little instruction, which they gave me easily and without embarrassment. They were tolerant of errors, but Bembang watched me like a hawk, and told on me when I inadvertently pulled up a useful plant. I got out my camera and took pictures of Bangkang and Caya who responded by striking funny poses with their sprayers, again amidst much hilarity.

Caya had on an old, but very beautifully worked sunhat made of rattan, woven into lovely Iban designs. I admired it, and they told me I should buy one. I said I would love to if I could find someone willing to sell one. They were pretty sure someone at the longhouse was making one and that I would be able to get it. Buying things from Dayaks is usually a difficult and embarrassing proposition, since they are unwilling to name a price and/or are often uninterested in selling their handiwork. Still I hoped I might indeed be able to get a lovely hat like that.

As we worked, Injan began good-naturedly pestering me to sing. I'm not at all clever at singing, but---probably since I'd drunk half a cup of *arak* before I had any food---I obliged. I sang "Rock a Bye Baby," explaining that this song was to put your children to sleep. They laughed with delight. Did I have any songs to put your husband to sleep? More laughter. Then they wanted sad songs. They wanted to cry because their husbands were gone. I sang as much as I could remember of "Sentimental Journey" and "Hang Down Your Head, Tom Dooley." They seemed pleased, but when we all urged Injan to sing, she said she was too sad, and would sing another time. Today she wanted to hear these foreign songs. I don't think my "sad songs" brought on any tears though.

When we took a break, resting in the shade by the path, Bembang ran over to the fieldhut and brought back a gourdful of lovely fresh water from a nearby stream. Injan and Mni' began discussing adultery. Injan said that if anyone took away her husband, she'd kill the woman. It is not, incidentally, at all uncommon for a Dayak husband to take another wife in Malaysia. Sometimes they never come home. I asked if the Iban didn't fine people, like the Kenyah do, for adultery. No, they said, the aggrieved wife is allowed to kill the adulteress. I still take this piece of information with a grain of salt, wondering if it was a mildly veiled threat lest I had designs on their husbands. But taking another woman's husband is not allowed. What happens away from home does not concern them, they agreed---just so they didn't know about it.

Mni' spoke nostalgically of how her husband would massage her body or in some other unspecified way make her forget her pains and fatigue after a hard day of weeding in the ricefield. They kept talking of being cold without their men. I'd heard this idea before, but it still strikes me as hard to comprehend in an environment where the outside temperature is almost always 90 degrees during the day, and only slightly cooler at night! Much of their talk was a sort of eulogy to marital pleasure. I was surprised because the Kenyah women I'd worked with would have been embarrassed to acknowledge their longing for their absent husbands in this direct way (though it was clear that they too missed them).

I'd been with my newfound friends for several hours when Injan laughed and told me how frightened she had been when she'd seen me the first time near her field. She said she had thought I was a killer. If she had indeed thought that, she was a remarkably brave woman, as she hadn't even flinched when I fell in step with her, and accompanied her home. They had all been afraid of me, they agreed, but when I sang for them, most of their fear had vanished. Before I left, delighted with the afternoon, both personally and professionally, Mni' handed me some squash leaves as a gift.

Counterparts - in Brief

In September, Pak Tori took over from Pak Toto as head of the Conservation Agency (CA) in Pontianak. Pak Tori was a highly sophisticated and intelligent, western trained scientist with an unusual knack for dealing assertively with westerners. We liked him very much but this hadn't stopped us from haranguing him for the promised counterparts on every possible occasion. In early November, Dudley came back from one of his trips to Pontianak in search of funds, with a whole slew of Indonesian CA staff members.

Three of them constituted a team, reportedly newly trained by Pak Tori in the use of the GPS (or Global Positioning System)---I was very excited to see the first item of our promised "equipment." Could there be more coming? This team's task: To check up on the condition of the posts which were reported to mark the boundaries of the Reserve.

This was a funny story in itself. We had, on various occasions, gone out looking for these posts which we'd been told had been put up the previous October. We'd only been able to locate two in our cursory searches. We'd also been trying much more seriously to find out the legal boundaries of the reserve. But no one could find the right map. In the search we found several maps, with differing borders and differing reserve statuses. The one with the most official signatures referred to our area as a "Strict Nature Reserve" (or *Cagar Alam*), not a "Wildlife Reserve" (*Suaka Margasatwa*). I fervently hoped this was not the map we were looking for, partly because of the differing implications for people living within the reserve. Technically people were not allowed to live in either kind of reserve, but the government's enforcement was likely to be much more stringent in a Strict Nature Reserve. Our whole project---and my interest in it---was built on the idea of working cooperatively with the several thousand people living in and around the reserve. The arrival of this team---here to check on the boundary markers---must surely mean that someone had found the map used in putting them out. Surely this would be the real map!

As the team was piling out of the speedboat into the Buaya Biru II, Dudley spied the GPS. He has an eternal fascination for high tech gadgetry. "How does it work?" He asked. The team members exchanged embarrassed glances. One busied himself unpacking the box of batteries needed to run it, one searched for the instruction manual, one looked at the floor. No one answered. Dudley recognized this behaviour. He rephrased the question: "Do you know how to use it?"

"No," came the instantaneous and unanimous response.

"But I thought you just finished a training course..."

"Yes, but Pak Tori was very busy, and....well, we didn't really understand..."

My husband, amazing man that he is, took the instruction manual, figured out how to use this strange device, and taught the team the skills they needed. In the course of this training, we learned two memorable things: One was that these CA high school graduates did not know that the Equator was on 0° latitude. The other was the kind of "map" they'd been given to check the boundary markers. It consisted of several pieces of typing paper taped together. On this paper was a nearly vertical straight line, topped by another straight line veering off to one side. The presence of three rivers which we could surmise were the Kapuas, the Tawang and the Kenelang were the only indicators of context on the sheets.

On inquiry we learned from the quite charming, young, would-be surveyors that the office in Sintang where they'd gotten the "map" had been quite reluctant to give them anything. When the team had persisted, they had been provided with this minimal information. Because CA had a budget to check only a few kilometers, the office had given them "only a few kilometers" of map.

We did learn from this experience that the boundary markers had been put well within the borders of the smallest area we had considered possible for the reserve. Why, we did not know. Had powerful timber interests put pressure on forestry officials to minimize reserve size? Was there yet another reserve map? Or was it simply laziness on the part of the earlier surveyors who placed the markers in easily accessible areas? Impossible to ascertain without a great deal of detective work.

Meanwhile two other counterparts had arrived with the survey team. One was Agus, a college graduate from a sister agency within the Forestry Department; the other was Didin, a big burly high school graduate from CA. Agus explained that he could not stay with us long term, but he would be returning for a couple of weeks every month or two. Didin was to remain with us as the first of our long-awaited, long-term counterparts. What a welcome surprise!

Since the Field Center was not yet operational, An, one of our boat drivers, offered his mother's home. We were pleased with this arrangement since it would give Agus and Didin a chance to get to know community members, as well as providing a small source of additional income to An's widowed mother.

Our first hint of trouble came during Dudley's GPS mini-course. Agus, Didin and An were all invited to participate in the course and readily accepted the invitation. But Didin, who showed no outstanding brilliance himself, began making fun of An whenever possible. To avoid embarassing Didin, I took both him and Agus aside, explaining the importance of maintaining good relations with community members and how dependent we were on our drivers' good will. No effect. I then gave my own mini-course on working with communities, and gave each of them a practice task to do. Still no effect. Everyone noticed that whenever we got into a speedboat, Didin fell asleep. Indeed, he seemed to be asleep a good bit of the time. At least asleep, he was doing no harm!

Meanwhile An was looking more and more glum. He finally asked for my help, saying that his mother could not afford to keep them any longer. I learned then that they had not been contributing to household food costs. Instead, Didin had treated An's mother like his personal servant. I immediately spoke with Didin and helped arrange for him to stay in an empty office building. He assured me he would move there promptly, and Agus left for a few days to do a mini-study in Sekolat.

I was surprised when An's mood did not improve. It was several days before I learned that Didin was still living at An's house, still contributing nothing to subsistence, and still treating community members in an arrogant and patronizing manner. Dudley and I agonized over what to do. We'd waited for months for our CA counterpart, yet we finally agreed that the project was better off with no one than with this fellow. We sent him back to Pontianak---anxious about Pak Tori's reaction, but seeing no real alternative.

A couple of months later we learned that Didin had run amok in the CA office in Pontianak, destroying a number of important computer diskettes and throwing a co-worker's motorcycle into a ditch. We felt we'd been wise to send him home. When we got no negative feedback from Pak Tori, we suspected that CA had simply tried to get rid of a troublesome employee by sending him upriver. We never saw the very capable and likable Agus again.

Excitement on Lake Seriang

Our first home in Pulau Majang was near the mouth of the Majang River, in a fairly direct line, East Northeast of the main landing area for the village. This location was convenient, since we could paddle quickly to anyplace in town. The main drawback came with the occasional high winds and resulting waves.

One day in November, I had been feeling a bit under the weather. The discovery that I had a mild fever was enough to convince me to bathe, don a sarong, remove my contacts, and settle in for the night. Just as I was getting comfortable, the wind began to pick up. It was only a very short time before the winds began truly to rage, and I decided I had better get up and put my contacts back on (since I am totally useless without them).

While engaged in this mundane task, there came a sudden, loud crrruuunch, and Buaya Biru I suddenly began lurching wildly back and forth, threatening to smash the shingles off the roofs of both Buaya Biru (BB) I and II. Some of the poles that held the boats apart had come loose. Dudley rushed to the door at the mid-section, and held off BBI. By this time, I had one contact on, and he asked me in a carefully controlled voice, into which I sensed considerable urgency, if I didn't have my contacts on yet. I worked faster. Just as I got the second contact in, there came another ominous sound. Our lab boat, Rancong

Loncat, which was tied to the other side of BB II, had also come loose, and was beginning to heave wildly from side to side as well.

Dudley yelled to me to go into the lab boat (something of an acrobatic feat under the best of circumstances, which this certainly was not) and bring back some tires to use as bumpers. Realizing that my sarong would doubtless drop at an inconvenient and possibly dangerous moment, I stepped out of it, and hastened over to the other boat in the buff. Well, events picked up speed as I rushed nude from boat to boat, bringing rope and tires while trying to hold the Lab boat away from BBII. Meanwhile, Dudley continued to hold BBI and BBII apart, while tying on extra ropes and tires.

He finally looked at me and opened his mouth to say something; then he changed his mind and closed it again. From our years of marriage, I was able to surmise from this that he would prefer I took a moment to put on some clothes. By then it was indeed possible to take that luxury. We spent the next 45 minutes standing on opposite sides of BBII, keeping our tire bumpers in place, and holding off Rancong Loncat and BBI, respectively, until the wind and waves dropped back to normal. Concerns about my mild fever were completely obliterated by the adrenalin high engendered by these events.

We spent the next hour or so, making sure the boats were again securely tied together, so that we could go to bed with some measure of confidence. While Dudley tied, retied, and adjusted poles, I cut and burned the ends of strips of the strange but strong polypropelene line we used. We then had to go out into the night, still pouring down rain, and bail out the armada we maintained tied to our home. That night our additional fleet consisted of two longboats and three canoes. All were full of water. When this last task was done, we treated ourselves to some of the tastiest hot chocolate I have ever enjoyed.

Unreasoning Fear

One night in late November, when I went to spend a night in Empaik, I was again struck by strange fears. I had met with the whole community to discuss the work I wanted to do there. I wanted them to fill out some forms on a daily basis for me. In the middle of the meeting, five of their men unexpectedly returned from Malaysia, where they had been working. Our meeting stopped, and the party began. They got out a case of *arak* (the potent rice liquor), and after some preliminary niceties, began to drink. Over the next few hours, the longhouse (some 40 adults) managed to drink the entire case.

I had been ill the previous few days, so using that as an excuse I was reluctantly allowed to stop drinking and retreat to my sleeping mat. As the revelry continued around me, my foolish fears began to surface. They all laughed and shouted and cavorted playfully, running up and down the longhouse, singing, popping into the apartment where I was feigning sleep, inviting me to come out again. Once when a group came in, they began to argue, and I feared they might come to blows. I played the peacemaker for the teacher, who was acting superior, and a woman who felt he wasn't. One man almost punched another, but was restrained by his comrades.

Finally they left me to try to sleep. But my heart continued to pound wildly. I remembered my Melayu neighbors' warnings that their main concern about my going to Empaik was Iban behavior when drunk. I remembered that the Iban had been ferocious warriors and headhunters, and I began to imagine they would forget themselves in their drunken revelry, and come for my head. I had lived and worked with the Kenyah for over a year, and never felt such fears. I remain at a loss to explain them. These people always treated me well.

The Bureaucrats Come to Call

In late November, a review was scheduled. A team from the Indonesian Conservation Agency, the British ODA, SCF, and TLI would be coming to see the Wildlife Reserve and what we had been up to. Getting them all upriver and finding them a place to eat and sleep, particularly when the Field Center was not yet ready for occupancy, was a tactical nightmare. Still I hoped that their visit might result in some speedup in getting the long awaited equipment and perhaps they might even help in getting us the rest of the project's personnel. We were still working alone except for our boat drivers and occasional community members.

I had some trepidation about the ability of these bureaucrats to adapt to our living conditions. Would they be able to traverse the planks over water? Could they cope with the bland, boring diet? What would they do when they realized there were no bathing facilities other than the rivers and lakes? We tried to warn them in a memo, but we knew it wouldn't all sink in until they arrived. In the back of my mind was the hope that being in the field with us, they might realize the importance of getting us some of that equipment! They might even do something about getting our budget and work plan---finished with such haste the previous June---approved.

The first full day, we scheduled a ride from Pulau Majang to Bukit Tekenang by longboat. In this way, we reasoned, they could see the flora and fauna, and also assess the progress on the Field Center, which was nearing completion. Dudley piloted one longboat in which, Steve, the young economist, John, an older forester and I rode. John was a colorful fellow, missing a front tooth or two and wearing a brightly colored lifejacket during the whole visit. He couldn't swim! While he regaled me with tales of his youthful treks in other remote areas of the world, Steve sat in front of us, staring down at his fingernails. 'Alan sat in the bow reading a book. Dudley had a clear view of us all, and noted that no one had paid the slightest bit of attention to the environment through which we were passing.

We had arranged for the Rancong Loncat, our lab boat, to pick up the whole group in Bukit Tekenang at about 11 and take us to Nanga Pengembung where we would have lunch. In this way, they could see how local people lived, and have a chance to talk with them. Habiba cooked a nice meal, and I offered to translate for anyone who wished to tour the village. Only Mary Jane, the social scientist on the team, expressed any interest in doing this, and even she was sated in a very short time.

We had planned for the Rancong Loncat---a rather slow craft---to go directly back to Pulau Majang, taking perhaps two hours. But Wim, in his usual fashion, decided without discussion that the team would like to take a longer route back. We wound up chugging down the Tawang and back up the Kenelang River, "so they could see more of the Reserve." When we got back home at 5 that afternoon, we were all exhausted and hoarse from conversing in voices loud enough to be heard over the very loud chug chug chug of the diesel engine.

The next day, I took Mary Jane to Empaik. As we crossed Lake Seriang, we had a chance for some real woman-to-woman talk. I had begun genuinely to miss conversation with women of my own age, culture, and education. I welcomed this chance to talk with another Western woman----just simple talk of children and work and places we'd lived, men we'd loved. It was a very nice little break.

Mary Jane was more buxom than most people in the Lakes area and she was unused to the continual balancing act that life in the Reserve constituted. Her difficulties were cause for much hilarity among local community members. They soon realized that she could not understand what they said, so they felt at liberty to make all sorts of rude remarks, requiring all of my wits when called on to translate.

It was with both relief and humor when we saw them all off for their trip downriver. We weren't at all sure that they would be able to expedite the equipment or the arrival of our other team members, all of which we had really ceased to expect. But we had all lived through the review, and assumed we would now be free to get on with our work once again.

Not so. Each of the review team members had a different idea of what we ought to be doing, and they made no effort to coordinate their ideas. As a result Dudley had to spend a couple of weeks in Pontianak and Jakarta trying to incorporate some of their suggestions into a revised work plan. We all agreed that the original work plan had been over-ambitious for the full team which was to include 4-8 Indonesian scientists, three more foreigners, and a number of short term consultants. It was really absurd to add tasks for a team reduced to two scientists without equipment and often without funds! And no progress was being made on getting approval for our budget or for our planned co-workers.

Suara Bakakak

We were relaxing in our boats one evening when Dudley suddenly turned to me and said "Why don't you publish a community newsletter? There's so little for local people to read; there'd be a big demand." I was hesitant at first. I knew I'd have to take primary responsibility for it, and I already had too much to do, but...it was an interesting idea.

I played around a little with the concept. A newsletter should belong to the community. We should definitely not simply be preaching at them about conservation. It would have to feature articles that grew out of the people's own conservation concerns. We could interview local people with expertise related to wildlife. There could be "letters to the editor" from local folks. We could sponsor and advertise conservation-related contests. Including informative articles on which species were protected---and on reserve boundaries if we could ever figure out where they were!---would appeal to CA and LTI. The more I thought about it the better I liked the idea. Dudley and I discussed some possible articles, and I began drafting them. Pak Markan and An corrected my grammar. Pak Sahar wrote a contribution.

We hashed the idea out at length. What would be a good name for such a newsletter? How about the *bakakak*, which zoomed across the rivers with remarkable regularity, its psychedelic blue plumage flashing in the sun? There was an interesting local myth about this bird. Pak Sahar suggested the black and white *Tinjau* (probably a flycatcher-shrike, *Hemipus sp.*). In the end we agreed that calling it *Suara Bakakak* (The Voice of the Stork-billed Kingfisher) would reflect our local concerns; we hoped the newsletter would actually become a voice for local people. We published our first issue in December, and it elicited enough local interest to keep us producing it on a monthly basis.

Rats in the Belfry

One day in November, I was meandering toward the bow of Buaya Biru I, when I saw the top of my son's red satin Chinese pyjamas (something he rarely wore) wrapped around a support frame in the hull. I was puzzled, and remember thinking "I know he's messy, but this is ridiculous." As I began pulling out the satin night shirt, I discovered bits of leaves, a teenager's colorful shoestring, and other odds and ends. Gradually the light dawned that a small animal---other than my son---was responsible for this. As I slowly and gingerly pulled out these trophies, wedged between the horizontal and vertical support beams which formed the boat's frame, I began to hear tiny little squeaky voices. At this point, I reasoned that my husband, being a biologist, was better qualified to deal with wildlife than I, so I requested his assistance. He was busy.

The next day, he discovered the new nest, complete with five naked baby mice, under the floor boards of Buaya Biru I. We extracted them and after some discussion reluctantly threw them overboard. We weren't sure it was legal drowning animals in a Wildlife Reserve! The mother, however, remained out of reach---though we occasionally caught glimpses of her, zooming by above our heads.

In December, just before we went back to the US, we got the first of our long-term team members. Ian Hood was a young wildlife biologist who had offered to work with us for his room and board for about six months. We were very happy to see him, and even more ecstatic as we realized what a find he was. He was hard-working, intelligent, committed---generally a delight! And he knew a lot about wildlife.

But to return to our furry friends. Before leaving DSWR, we carefully stowed the things we were afraid might be attacked by a mouse; and we left the boats in Ian's capable hands. Besides his general duties of monitoring wildlife in the Reserve, we gave Ian the added task of finding and removing the remaining mouse. Although he got two traps, and set them religiously, he too failed to catch her before having to go downriver---to Pontianak---on project business.

When we returned to our uninhabited boats in February, we found some amazing things. Most surfaces throughout both boats were covered with mouse droppings---small, (fortunately) hard, black tidbits. But we also found some quite unusual things had been eaten: The wooden sheath of a bush knife had a huge hole gnawed in it. The edges had been chewed off a number of the Tupperware-like containers in which we had stored food and other items. The insulation, and the *wire* it surrounded, had been eaten from my husband's toolbox. We found an empty tube of Cortisone cream, and Ian told us about a bottle of sweetened soy sauce being drained in one night. They ate the edges off my *American Anthropologist Newsletter*, but declined to eat the nearby books. They also ate part of the box in which the Bible my grandfather had given me was stored. My son's mosquito net developed a number of mysterious holes, as did the red satin pajama tops that first alerted us to the mouse's presence. One of the saddest losses was a lovely photograph that I had carefully turned upside down, and covered with other paper to protect. Mouse urine somehow made its way to one corner of the picture, making a peculiar pink stain on the otherwise cream colored cardboard frame.

We adjusted to these losses, none too serious. But after our return, we had other problems with our 'pet mouse.' We often heard strange sounds in the night, things falling down, unexplained crashes and bangs. One day I found two (chicken) eggs which had been removed from their storage tray; another day the leftover French bread I had carefully stored in a plastic bag for later (human) consumption disappeared.

One morning my son awoke with blood all over his big toe. We all assumed he'd stubbed his toe without realizing it--not at all uncommon, since he is often in a world of his own. I carefully washed his toe, revealing a tiny puncture wound, and applied a band-aid. A few nights later, I was awakened in the night out of a sound sleep by a sharp yelp from my husband. He indignantly told me that something had bitten him. We found our flashlights, and peered through the gloom at his big toe. Sure enough blood was flowing freely from a small, familiar-looking puncture wound. Apparently our pet mouse had climbed up our mosquito net, and found my husband's toe (like my son's) a tasty morsel, conveniently positioned against the net. She just took a little bite. Getting back to sleep proved to be a little problematic, as I lay there wondering when my turn would come. After my husband's attack, I found myself sleeping in a ball, keeping my feet well away from the net.

But there was another chapter in the mouse saga. 'Alan awoke again with a puncture wound and blood all over his toe, this time, his second toe. The same day we found a rather cute creature, scurrying around and wiggling her (?) nose, in our live mouse trap. We got out *Mammals of Borneo* to identify her, and decided she was almost certainly *Rattus rattus*. Our mouse was a rat! After some deliberations, we decided to drop her overboard. 'Alan took the cage into our canoe, moored against the Buaya Biru II, and released her. To my surprise, with great agility and apparent delight, she swam away from the boats as fast as she could go, turned left behind them, head visible above the water surface, and dog-paddled away into the bushes. She, or her friends, returned, and though we overcame some of our distaste for killing them, we never again managed to divest ourselves or our unusual home of these vampire rats.

Project Problems

When we left DSWR in December, I was exhausted. The lifestyle was physically tiring of course, but more draining were continuing problems dealing with TLI and SCF. I couldn't understand why project funds couldn't be sent to Pontianak where we could get them in a timely manner, as planned and as needed. TLI blamed SCF; SCF blamed TLI. We had paid for project expenses with our own money on several occasions, rather than leave local employees and contractors unpaid. There seemed to be no progress on the equipment; it was beginning to look as though the volunteer team members might not get visas after all; no Indonesian counterparts had been assigned except for the two who came for two week visits and never returned. We were in too remote an area to follow up on these things ourselves, and we couldn't find out where the problems lay. I also wondered about our salaries. When asked, Wim had said several times that we were being paid but always in a rather peculiar and tentative way. Wim had asked us to come through the home office in December to meet with him and other TLI staff, and we looked forward to straightening out some of these problems then.

But this was not to be. On arrival in Pontianak in early December, a fax was waiting for us: Wim and TLI's administrator would be at a regional meeting elsewhere during our visit. Hmmm. So much for that idea.

Our air tickets were for the next day. It would have been hard to change our plans at that point. And anyway, we needed the proof of money transfers to figure out our finances with our bank in the US. Shortly after our arrival, we went into TLI's accounting office, where sat their jolly old accountant. We sat down, and exchanged greetings. He smiled at us, and handed us the papers we had requested. We looked at them, a bit nonplussed. "These are only the transfers from June and the first week of July, before we went on leave. Where are the rest?" A fake smile was plastered on his face, as he chuckled nervously. "Heh heh, that's all there are." And that was indeed all there were.

I was flabbergasted....and enraged. I kept thinking, if we'd had a home we were making payments on like most people, our home would have been repossessed without our ever knowing it---and these people we worked for wouldn't even have cared. We were working very hard, trying to do the best we could on a job we felt was vitally important, and this was our reward. It was really unthinkable.

We went back to the US and enjoyed Christmas. We refused to return to Indonesia until we were provided with pre-paid tickets and some of our back pay was received in the US. But when we did return, it was with considerable skepticism about what lay before us.

In mid-January, we stopped at the home office on our way back to DSWR. Dudley offered to share his user-friendly bookkeeping program with LTI's staff and teach them how to use it. They were doing the bookkeeping by hand; the offer was ignored.

There we learned that the volunteers would not receive visas from the Indonesian government and thus could not join us in the field. Ian Hood---who had made wonderful progress on wildlife monitoring and had helped develop an excellent hunting survey---was being kicked out of the country, because he had come upriver to work with us "under false pretenses." We were never quite sure what the problem really was, but he seemed to have rubbed a senior official the wrong way. We suspected something as innocuous as wearing informal dress to the office or using the project car when the official wanted it.

And copies of the review team's remarks were finally available: The ecologist basically wrote a new work plan which he added to the old one, telling us to work more with various governmental agencies. The social scientist, with whom I'd thought I was communicating, said that we should have jumped even more immediately into participatory action---presumably without funds or personnel! Her accusation that we were paying local people to cooperate---particularly ironic in light of our problems even getting money to pay our boat drivers' salaries---seemed a double betrayal. It was ludicrous...and even more disheartening.

'Alan as Pariah

One day in February, while Dudley was again in Pontianak seeking project funds, 'Alan came home in a blue funk. It wasn't long before I learned that all his friends, including his nearest and dearest, were suddenly afraid to play with him. They told him, sadly, that the teacher had told them that playing with him was *haram* (forbidden under Islamic law), and that those who played with him would not pass to the next grade in school. My contribution: Sympathy and the suggestion that he wait a day or two, that the admonition had probably never been made and would surely soon lose its force.

But several days passed, and he remained comparatively isolated. Being a gregarious soul, this was hard on him. I tried to help by going up to the boardwalk in the afternoons to watch him play badminton, hoping my presence would remind the community that we were a human family despite our (non-practicing) Christianity.

Finally one morning, when a slightly older child who braved the injunction against playing with 'Alan confirmed the story quite convincingly, I sought out the teacher to try to find out what was going on. He was on a raft, near our boat, bathing in his underwear---not unusual attire for men of the lakes. I apologized for interrupting his bath, and said the children had told me that he was forbidding them to play with 'Alan, that 'Alan was *haram*. Was this true?

He smiled at me in a friendly enough fashion, his nervousness only betrayed by his badly shaking hands---interacting with Westerners is inherently stressful for most people here, until they really get to know you. He explained that the children were neglecting their religious duties, not going to pray at 6 PM (*sholat*) as they were supposed to, because they continued to play with 'Alan.

I acknowledged that their duty to pray was a significant concern (and I did not mention that in fact 'Alan had to be, and normally was, home by dark---just about 6 PM). But I also expressed my view that teachers should not teach young children to hate other people because of religion (common, but strictly forbidden in the Indonesian government philosophy). He quickly denied ever forbidding the children to play with 'Alan, reiterating that they were only forbidden to play when it was time to pray. He did mention, however, with some pride, that the Indonesian children, unlike 'Alan, were "afraid of" him.

We parted on friendly terms, with my offering to try to teach 'Alan to be a little more blatantly respectful of adults (as required by Indonesian custom), while he reassured me that he did not consider interacting with Christians to be bad. I understood that he was going to explain to the children more precisely that they could play with 'Alan when it was not prayer time.

This interaction is typical. I still don't know exactly what really happened, and unfortunately never will. The teacher's words cannot be taken at face value. The fact that 'Alan was normally home by *sholat* prayer time suggests that this was not the real problem; his lack of fear of the teacher may have been.

Fears Again

Again the fears surfaced. My husband was still in Pontianak, 'Alan and I alone in our boats. The religious controversy was just resolved, when a new problem surfaced. 'Alan borrowed a badminton racket and was playing with it apparently innocently on someone's front porch, when the homeowner came out, grabbed the racket from 'Alan's hand and broke it over his knee, loudly expressing his anger that the children were playing on his porch. We later learned that, unbeknownst to 'Alan, the homeowner had warned the children not to play there. In subsequent days there was a whispering campaign to persuade us to pay for the racket. I did not think this made sense; it seemed to me that the man who broke the racket should pay for it.

While the controversies about the rackets and religion raged in the village, I lay in my bed at night, unable to sleep, listening to the regular creaking of the boat, the wind whistling through it, the scratchings of insects and rats---and imagined robbers and rapists and people ready to cut off our heads. I remembered that the phrase, "to run amok," is originally from the language of these Melayu people among whom I lived. The verbal form is *ngamok.*

I have been blessed, most of my life, with a virtual absence of fear. The wildly beating heart, the ears maximally tuned and listening for strange sounds, eyes seeking out unusual light patterns that might warn of intruders (animal, human, or spirit), the mind turning over every violent possibility---these have been rare sensations for me. But I even began to remember the warnings about magic in Borneo. I wondered in the night if I had been naive all these years to disregard them. Were those howls (probably cattle) really ghosts or spirits seeking out human victims? Such strange thoughts came to my mind, alone in the dark of the night.

Tippy Canoe

How affected we all are by the weather! The heat spell broke and the rains returned, bringing with them delightfully cool temperatures, so much more hospitable to human needs and frailties. With the drop in temperature there was an obvious rise in everyone's spirits.

Entering a little data, reading a little from *Walking among the Great Apes* (seeking inspiration perhaps?), cooking English muffins---I'd had a thoroughly relaxing day. At about 4, relaxing by my open door, I noted that 'Alan and three of his friends were coming back in his canoe in the pouring rain, from checking their fish lines. They looked so happy and yet so dripping, I decided to take their picture. Returning only a few seconds later with my camera, I was shocked to see only their heads barely visible above the water...and there was no sign of 'Alan's canoe! I called to them several times asking if they were in trouble, did they need help? They didn't look happy....and they didn't answer. I decided caution was the better part of valor in this case, so I quickly untied my own canoe, and headed out after them.

Someone had leaned to the left when he should have leaned to the right, and the boat had capsized. They hadn't heard me calling. 'Alan knew some canoes were made from sinker wood and he was afraid his canoe wouldn't float, capsized. He thought his father would kill him if he sank his canoe---hence the worried look. Although not in any danger, they greeted me with considerable gratitude. Together, looking more and more like drowned rats with every paddle stroke, we slowly made our way to shore---my canoe, 'Alan's canoe floating full of water, his floorboards and paddles, plus me and four boys of varying sizes. Three of the boys swam in the water, working to keep the sunken (and therefore very unwieldy) canoe somewhat parallel to mine. Another boy and I paddled, trying our best not to hit the swimming boys with our paddles, while making slow forward progress toward the shore.

Once ashore, they all leaped happily to the task of wildly rocking 'Alan's canoe from side to side. I was surprised how quickly and effectively they could empty it of water; and I was free to make a much quicker and more direct trip back to the boat (and dry clothes).

Sitting quietly alone in my boat, watching the rain hit the water, I remembered some of the delights this environment holds. Raindrops were dropping onto the water's surface, making round splashes, rippling outward in concentric circles, and making the grey and silver water look alive. It was such a contrast to the view the previous afternoon---absolutely still waters, black as the black of night, making perfect mirror-like reflections of the boats, the trees, even the clouds above. The same red dragonflies flit about whether it rains or not.

Getting Ashore

We moved our boats, in February to a new location a ways up the Majang River, in an area which was quiet, solitary, and surrounded by partially inundated trees. We could hear birds and frogs and other natural sounds much of the day and night. And we were protected from the wind and waves. But getting ashore was considerably more complicated than it had been at our last mooring. We would paddle our canoes up to the boardwalk which was being extended further back behind the village. Standing in the bow of the canoe, the boardwalk just about reached my neck---at first. Since I was unable to swing my body up to the boardwalk, my husband hammered a small step into the post supporting the boardwalk. I could, with difficulty, hike myself up to the boardwalk using this step. However, later the water level went down. I had to park my canoe farther out, picking my way through the water, seeking logs, tree stumps, floating bits of debris on which I might balance, as I maneuvered through the mud to the end of the boardwalk. There was a convenient tree stump onto which I could climb to reach the framework of the unfinished boardwalk. I then had to hoist myself onto a 10 cm x 10 cm crossbeam, which in turn was topped with a tippy plank along which I could totter to reach the more secure footing of the completed boardwalk.

The walk along the boardwalk of Pulau Majang was normally comparatively uneventful. The community maintained its boardwalks in pretty good condition, so I did not have to fear, as I did in Ng. Pengembung, that I was about to break through a rotten board or fall into a hole, with every step. One day that I remember well, I got to the 'restaurant' where we took our meals, and discovered the door bolted (not an unusual occurrence). The solution to this dilemma was simply to use the upstairs door. But getting there required walking up creaky wooden steps to a ledge of about 40 cm in width, along the front of the building, on the second floor. Neither the stairs nor the ledge had a railing. Unlike local people who scamper up the stairs and happily run along this narrow ledge without apparent fear for life or limb, I would make my way slowly and carefully, grasping the sides of the wall at every opportunity, expecting to crash down to the boardwalk below with each step.

The *piece de resistance* was the dinner, the bulk of the food always rice. This rice might be supplemented by three pieces (one each) of dried fish, salted fish, boiled fish, fish in a hot sauce, fried fish, smoked fish, ground fish patties, or fried patties made of whole baby fish. There might also be a small bowl of ground cassava leaves, boiled squash or boiled cucumbers. Once in a while, we would get three tiny pieces of tough fried chicken, or three eggs in chili sauce, or even a bowl of fried noodles to go with our rice. But the part of the meal that made it all worthwhile was.....the water. They served clear rainwater, with ice. Sometimes the water was all that my son managed to get down! The water we drank in our boat, we drew with a bucket from the lake and boiled. Although it was probably germ free by the time we drank it, it still retained the color characteristic of blackwater lakes---for the sake of politeness, I'll say it was reminiscent of weak tea. None of us ever quite got accustomed to drinking water of this color.

To return to the day in question, after eating my supper of rice, fried noodles, and two pieces of chicken (my husband was away, so I got his), I returned to my canoe, which I had parked in a new place. I'd managed to find my way among the mass of semi-submerged bushy trees, to the boardwalk closer into town, where I had spied a real ladder, reaching down into the water. I had brought my canoe in, hopped out onto a conveniently placed log, tied up my canoe, and noted smugly that I was "home free."

Well, reversing this process, getting back to our boats, proved a little more difficult. First someone else had parked their canoe between mine and the log. This required my stepping into their even tippier canoe, to reach my own. I untied my canoe, balancing all the while (with expensive camera in fanny pack), and shoved off. I shoved off again...and again. I poked the ground and nearby stumps with my paddle. Stuck! I got out of my canoe, into my neighbors', and waggled and wiggled and juggled my canoe until it came free. Again I got in my own canoe, and eventually managed to extricate myself from this shallow portion of Danau Seriang. I realized it was getting dark. I tried to hurry a bit, making my way to the shortcut I had used to get to town. I saw the straight shot through the trees, and headed for it.

The trip began well enough...but just as I was beginning to relax, I came to a dead end, a solid wall of bushy trees. Turn back---aaaah, not so easy. The trees were closer together than the length of my canoe, and I was not yet an expert canoe handler anyway. I backed into the trees on one side of the pathway, and my bow got stuck in the trees on the other side. Two young boys passed me by, managing their canoes with consummate skill, smiling at me, never realizing how hopelessly entangled I was in these bushes. I extricated myself, and got stuck again, time and again. The sun was going down, and I was beginning to have minor feelings of panic. 'Alan had gone home the usual way. He'd be wondering what had happened to me, might even come out looking for me in the dark. He could get lost. Many such thoughts flashed through my mind. I cursed myself for not bringing a flashlight, and felt tears of frustration threatening.

But finally I managed to get out of the 'shortcut' area, and into the main lake. I'd wanted to avoid that because I had ample evidence of how fast the wind could come up, and I was leery of being blown away. But at least skirting the bushes, I could see where I was going, and get home. I made it just as the last bit of light began to fade. My son, thankfully still on board, greeted me with a cheery, 'Where were you, Mom?'

Fomenting Intervillage Fisheries Management

Although much of our early work had focused on research---both fisheries and community---the main purpose of our being at DSWR was to manage the Wildlife Reserve with local people. By early 1993, we knew one thing we would have to do: Get the fisherfolk together to determine regulations that they would agree to and help enforce.

We had gradually assembled a few more team members. Rimpun had joined us from the Conservation Agency; we had hired Luat as an Office Manager; and we'd come to rely more and more on our drivers, An and Markan, for substantive input. The six of us met at the nearly completed Field Center to decide the best way to get the fisherfolk together.

Based on our discussion, we divided the Reserve into five areas. We would assemble representatives from the villages along each of these four rivers and one lakeshore in separate meetings. The fisherfolk would bring and discuss maps of their areas and their existing regulations. Our goal for these meetings was for them to share their perceptions of fisheries-related problems, and to begin to agree on standard or at least mutually complementary regulations.

We decided to begin with the upper Tawang River, since this was the area we were most familiar with. As a first step, we asked Sahar from Nanga Pengembung, to accompany us to Genting, a nearby village. He and Sa'id were doing a survey of fisherfolk's perceptions of fisheries problems in several villages, and we could tag along to discuss the idea of these meetings with some fisherfolk, when they went to Genting.

Sahar, who like Markan, seemed to have relatives and friends everywhere, thought that an excellent idea. He said the people of Genting were still suspicious of us, and we should go there to straighten out their misconceptions. He also wanted to show us a fleet of his neighbors out fishing with *ambai*, a special kind of large dipnet. We would have to leave from Pulau Majang very early in the morning to catch them, but it would be well worth our seeing.

Dudley and I obediently arose and departed at about 5 AM, heading off in a *longbot* for Ng. Pengembung, our rendezvous point with Sahar and Sa'id. Being up and about at this hour was always a delight. The temperature was comfortable, there was mist in the air, the light on the water and the foliage was lovely, the birds were singing. I would always wonder why I didn't leave home earlier every day---though parental responsibilities were one significant reason.

We met Sahar and Sa'id, as planned, and headed off up the Pengembung River in search of the fisherfolk. We were dismayed, though not surprised, to encounter them one by one, all heading back to the village, with their colorful fishing gear carefully stowed. There hadn't been enough fish to continue their efforts. O well.

On we went, toward Lake Pengembung, which we would have to cross to get to the tiny hamlet of Genting. Genting's 200 or so inhabitants all lived on rafts or in *motor*s, arranged around the edges of a little bay, surrounded by the ubiquitous bushy trees. Arriving in the early morning, the village looked charming, each raft or boat with a backdrop of greenery reflected in the Lake's waters.

We went directly to the Head Fisherman's home, and the reason for Sahar's concern was immediately evident. That we were invited in and offered tea is a tribute to their courage. Their fear was palpable. We might have been alien spirits coming in search of their blood, from the way they looked at us. We got out copies of the most recent *Suara Bakakak*, and gave them some. We smiled a lot. We explained the project's goals. Gradually, gradually, they began to relax. Maybe we weren't there to find a virgin to sacrifice or to steal their children, after all.

Gradually we were able to bring the conversation around to the idea of a meeting of their community representatives with those of several other nearby communities. This didn't sound so threatening to them. In fact, they rather liked the idea. The longer we talked, the happier they looked.

Finally, just before we left, the Head Fisherman got up his nerve to ask about some of the more bizarre rumors he'd heard about us. We were surprised also to hear that we were to build a helicopter pad on Bukit Tekenang, and maybe even a bridge to span the lakes.

As we left his tiny home, we found a Brahminy Kite peacefully eating fish drying in the sun on the neighboring raft. Apparently a child had found it as a baby, and the people had raised the beautiful bird. It was completely unencumbered and free to go, but it chose to stay, where the food was plentiful. Although I knew that many ecologists disapprove even of this kind of relationship between people and animals, I felt this was a far happier way than tying the animal to rafts or putting them in cages. I said as much.

We headed for the Field Center with only one minor mishap along the way. Our engine got caught in a gillnet spread across the opening of a bay, and we had to spend quite a while carefully untangling it. Making holes in people's fishing nets was not a popular thing to do.

But I was happy with our morning. We had corrected some dangerous misconceptions in one community, and we had gotten positive feedback about our fisheries management ideas. We resolved to arrange the first meeting---just as soon as we could get the funds to DSWR!

Ramadan

Awakened out of a sound sleep at 3:30 AM, I remember...with a feeling of dread...that this is the first day of Ramadan, the holy Islamic fasting month. How would it affect our lives this year? The advent of loudspeakers has, in some settings, changed what was once a custom perfectly compatible with other systems of belief into a yearly ordeal for anyone not fasting.

The previous year, we lived on the outskirts of Pekanbaru (in Riau, Sumatra) across the street from one mosque, and surrounded at some distance by four others. All turned their loudspeakers on top volume. Naturally their messages were in no way synchronized. The result: An incredible cacophonous barrage of sound, frequently but intermittently from 3:30 AM one day until 1 AM the next. Eeeevery day. None of the several types of earplugs we tried could drown out the sound. We were literally driven from our home by exhaustion and irritability caused by...lack of sleep.

Here it was just beginning. The cool and beautiful morning calm was broken at 3:30 AM, first with the warning that there was only a half an hour more in which to eat breakfast. Then came Koranic readings, in both Arabic and Indonesian, until 4:16. Then the softer sound of drumbeats marked *Syuhur*, the true beginning of the fast.

The sound of one mosque is infinitely preferable to that of 5 in competition. The readings were nicely done, well modulated voices, microphones sufficiently distant from the speaker so that they did not distort their voices. Today and tonight would be the real tests. Would our neighbors also give speeches, sermons, Koranic readings, Islamic injunctions and reminders, from sunset until the wee hours of the morning, driving away sleep as they would drive away demons, sin, and other forbidden things? We would soon know.

The morning silence returned. The sky was full of brilliant stars, sprinkled across the heavens in their varying patterns. Here and there you could even see them reflected in the waters of the lake. Although we lived almost at sea level, it felt like the top of the highest mountain, so close were we to this vast and lovely array of lights. They could have been a blanket, yet they held no cloying closeness. Somehow rather than closing you in, this blanket of stars suggested infinity, infinite possibilities for beauty and truth. Mornings were definitely the best part of the day.

Ramadan in Pulau Majang turned out to be no problem at all!

Chapter V: Move Number Three – to Bukit Tekenang

In March, the waters began to recede. At the same time, our new facility at Bukit Tekenang was nearly finished, ready for occupancy. Once the waters really receded, our large boats wouldn't be able to navigate to and from Pulau Majang. We didn't want to get stuck there, and we did want to supervise the finishing touches on the Field Center. We decided to move yet again.

Exploring Bukit Tekenang

A busy day of work. Time for a rest at 3 PM. We had just moved from Pulau Majang to Bukit Tekenang. I hopped in my canoe, and headed north up the Tawang River to inspect and enjoy my new surroundings. Keeping to the left side of the river, I managed to stay in the shade much of the time. But once in a while I slipped up and drifted into the sun. The tropical heat would immediately strike. Quickly, I'd paddle to the left.

I went past a *jermal*---a huge stationery fishnet that blocks off a whole stream---that wasn't there last time I came. Its blue mesh made scallops above the water, reflected again in the water. As I paddled along its length, the blue mesh met grey, and became very tightly woven at the "business end" where the fish were actually caught. Later, the head fisherman told me this was being used to get small fish to feed people's caged snakeheads (*jelawat, Leptobarbus hoevenii*).

On I paddled, past three *lanting*s (raft-homes), the sun glinting off their brown and gold fiber walls, any possible monotony of the scene relieved by the colorful clothing hanging on lines and the tiny green garden plots, planted in rotting, floating logs. No sign of people, most were too sensible to be out at 3 PM!

Beyond the *lanting*s, I saw *tabung*, the bamboo traps set for the colorfully striped *ulang uli*, which were running. These, people would check in the evening. Everyone had set out traps for them, getting perhaps 200 fish in a night. Then, there were individual hooks tied to trees and bushes along the shore. Still farther on, I encountered a gill net stretched across a small 'bay.'

At the entrance to the bay there was a large tree, with dramatically contorted support roots, reflected in the still waters. I paddled past it, seeing birds, startled by my quiet paddling, flying from tree to tree, their voices raised perhaps in alarm. Slowing down, I saw the tail of a monkey as it jumped from one tree to another, behind a curtain of leaves. Stopping, sitting silently, I hoped to see him again. I even trained my camera on a lovely lighted part of the forest, and hoped he might pass there---but he had left or hidden himself in the foliage, perhaps to watch me as I would watch him.

Finally, I decided to head back. Out of the bay, into the Tawang River again. I crossed over to the other side, realizing this would mean paddling in the sun. But there were coves and bays here too that I wanted to explore. One intriguing watery possibility turned immediately into flooded forest, with trees so close together I couldn't maneuver my canoe. But this little side trip provided a few moments of comfort, out of the sun, and I saw glimpses of birds that I couldn't quite identify.

Back to the Tawang, past what looked like a lake, then back to the village of Bukit Tekenang again, hailed by the friendly people, from every *lanting* I pass. "Come and visit." "Where have you been?" "Where are you going?" A bit hot, I head home for a cool bath.

Dreary

I felt like I lived in a terrible swamp, full of disease, alive with disgusting creepy crawly things, hidden dangers around every bend. I discovered I had probably had a fever for over a month---every afternoon (my febrile nemesis in the tropics). The fever saps your strength, leaving you flaccid, loose like a rag. The sweat streams down your face with the slightest exertion---even typing! Lying absolutely still, after a cool bath, gives some brief respite---but only as long as you do not move. The things you want to do, those aspects of your life that contribute significantly to its meaning, must wait. You cannot operate as a normal human being, with energy and enthusiasm. You can only lie down, drained of strength, without vigor. You are no longer a strong, capable being; you are weak. Not a nice thought.

Harnessing the Timber Companies

We had a good handle on fisheries management issues. We had a plan, and it looked like it was going to work. But I also thought we needed a plan for working with the folks surrounding the reserve. These Iban practiced shifting cultivation, which was considered a definite no-no by the Indonesian government. I knew that the government's extremely negative view was a bit misguided. The Iban system was actually much more complex---and less damaging---than was widely understood. But one part particularly concerned us; we were gradually realizing just how important hunting was as a part of their subsistence base.

Iban agroforestry wasn't our only concern though. The area around the reserve---traditionally Iban lands---had also been doled out by the central government to timber companies. Although these companies were supposed to follow fairly reasonable forest management guidelines, there was no monitoring of their activities. They could and did take what they liked without paying any attention to issues of sustainability or conservation. Their relations with the Iban were, to my mind, marked by a peculiar mixture of accommodation and oppression.

An idea gradually grew in my mind. Why couldn't the Iban communities help enforce the government's policies? The people would need to know the government's forest management guidelines and the details of forest company contracts. And our project and officials in the Conservation Agency would have to back them up when controversies arose. But the Iban lived there all year long. They knew and loved their homeland, and cared what was happening to it. Who better to monitor the timber companies? The more I thought about this idea, the better I liked it. It was empowering.

Again I called together all available staff members to discuss the idea; I discussed it with local community leaders, with concerned, educated Dayaks in Pontianak and with my anthropological colleague and Iban expert, Reed Wadley. All seemed to agree that it would be controversial, but the pro's outweighed the con's.

Gradually we began integrating our concern with Iban wildlife management into this plan. I suspected that the Iban had indigenous knowledge and management practices related to hunting, just as the fisherfolk had traditional fisheries regulations. My need to study this question was hampered by transportation problems. Iban communities were scattered far up many tiny rivers, in a fanlike dispersal around the reserve. They were much harder to reach than the Melayu fishing communities.

So I made a different kind of plan. We would tap into a local resource. Iban communities were producing scores of under-employed young people with a high school education. We would identify a small number willing to form a volunteer Conservation Cadre. We would bring them to the Field Center periodically for training in data gathering, interview techniques, group dynamics, data analysis and report writing. Between training sessions with us, they would return to their villages, with specific tasks: To teach village members about the regulations that applied to the timber companies; to map their communities' traditional land use and boundaries; to learn about their village's indigenous knowledge and management of wildlife; to help organize a system for monitoring the timber companies; to develop a series of wildlife management scenarios acceptable to their communities; etc.

We decided it was doable, and should be done. I worked with P. T. Bakermas, a Dayak NGO out of Pontianak, to develop a proposal for a sub-contract to do much of this work, and sent it up up up....into the bottomless bureaucratic pit. Still no money, no approval, and very few staff members. Doing it would probably have to wait a little longer.

More Money Troubles

I was hoping Dudley would arrive from his most recent trip downriver on Tuesday. I wasn't really worried when he didn't show for two more days, until I saw his face. He'd gone to Pontianak again to get project money. Each time he went to Pontianak, he would send a fax letting TLI know what we would need two or three months in advance. And each time TLI would send less than we would need, usually about half. That meant that Dudley would have to make another trip much sooner than should have been necessary, wasting more time and money on useless travel.

But this time things were even worse. We needed the money even more than usual. The project had owed Haji Idui, our building contractor, $ 8,500 since he finished the Field Center in late December. This debt was a problem for him since he had workers to pay, and it was becoming an embarrassment on a project that was supposed to work cooperatively with local people. They'd been cooperative, why weren't we? We were anxious to start our community meetings quickly so we could make significant progress during this wet season. During the dry season, which could start any time, we wouldn't be able to bring people together. The waterways, on which we depended for transport, would dry up. Of course we also had our normal operating costs (fuel for the boats, salaries for personnel). But most important of all was the Indonesian custom of giving Muslim staff members---which covered almost all of our co-workers---a Hari Raya bonus of an extra month's salary at the conclusion of the fasting month. TLI had not even given us enough to pay their salaries, let alone give them Hari Raya bonuses.

Dudley had, again, taken money from our personal savings account to pay our co-workers' salaries and give them their bonuses, but this was a final straw for us. It was this event which prompted us to give the four months' notice required in our contracts. We said we'd rather stay, we enjoyed our work, but that we couldn't continue in this context where we could not keep our word or our commitments. If we could be assured a steady supply of money---of which there was in fact no particular shortage within the Conservation Component of the ODA project---to conduct the necessary activities, we would stay on. Otherwise, July would be our last month.

Respite in Bukit Tekenang

Bukit Tekenang, home of the Field Center, is really a lovely place. At dusk, as I headed back to our boats after dinner, I again noticed the beauty of these flooded forests, with their tangles of roots. These tangles, tree trunks, and the leaves of the low canopy, reflected in the black waters, give such scenes a strange, bizarre, unnerving quality. A few steps further and the view from the end of the long boardwalk to the water was magnificent. To the Northwest lay the mountains of Malaysia, silhouetted between shimmering pinks and golds---all that remains of the harsh tropical sun. The lovely colors appear in the sky and again, reflected in the waters below. To the Northeast, the gentle curve of the Tawang, with the temporarily abandoned raft-homes, dominated the immediate scene; in the distance lay more mountains. I realized that before we built the Field Center with its long boardwalk, the distant mountains were only visible from the steep slopes of Bukit Tekenang. I was seeing a view perhaps rarely seen, even by the inhabitants---who feared the hill as a place of spirits.

The silent village, the equally abandoned Field Center, meant a welcome respite for me. *Hari Raya*, the biggest holiday of the year, would be today or tomorrow---depending on the appearance of the moon. When the moon was seen, the Muslim fasting month, the holy month of Ramadan, would be over. All our neighbors had left to rejoin their families and friends in their larger home village of Selimbau. If I were doing normal anthropological work, I would need to attend these festivities---but such occasions are less important for my main task, natural resource management. I let myself take this time for quiet thought, a rare peace.

Maimun

The people here were just as friendly as the others we'd met. Our senior boat driver and friend, Markan, found a young woman, Ida, willing to do our laundry for us; so a few days after we moved here I went to visit her raft-home and meet her. She was out checking her gillnet, but her mother, Maimun, was there, and a young neighbor girl, Amoi.

I was particularly taken by Maimun. Both her house and her kitchen, though tiny huts on rafts, with fish cages separating the two small structures, were unusually clean and neat. All clothing was neatly folded on shelves, she had even put linoleum on the floor of her home.

About my age, she was working in her kitchen, making cookies in an oven made from a ring cut from the base of a fuel drum. She made fires below and above, and put the rolled, diamond shaped cookie dough between.

She welcomed me with a frank and friendly smile, asking me a few questions. Exuding an air of quiet self-confidence, though I was probably the first Westerner she had ever spoken with, she told me of her children and her husband and her work. Her husband lived in Jongkong (Markan's hometown on the Kapuas River), and her children were all grown. Her work was baking cookies to sell to her neighbors (ten for US$.50) and going fishing, like her daughter.

We discussed her tiny but thriving garden on a floating, half rotted log, our families, fishing, her fish cages, *Hari Raya*, clothes washing. She was an independent sort of person. She gave the definite impression of being industrious, intelligent, and... interesting.

After chatting a while and watching her work, I bought a bag of cookies. I remembered that 'Alan had used up all our baking soda. On a whim I asked if she used it in her cookies. Yes. Did she have any extra that I could borrow? Of course. She loaded me up with a month's supply. I thought at the time that she and I might become friends, and I looked forward to that. A few days later I learned from Markan that Maimun's daughter, Ida (our laundress), had a high school education, and would like to do office work for us if there were an opportunity.

Our Neighbors Visit

Not long after we moved to Bukit Tekenang, I went back to the US. I had been suffering from a mild fever every afternoon for several months, and we decided that the time had come to do something about it. While I was gone, the Field Center at Bukit Tekenang changed from an empty shell to a functioning office, dormitory, and laboratory for the project. Project staff grew from just Dudley and me, with a speedboat driver and an occasional short termer, to a team of some twenty people. We welcomed the staff additions, but new people brought new problems. Our boats became even more of a haven for us.

Shortly after my return to Bukit Tekenang in late May, I was relaxing alone in the early evening in our boat. Although my strength had returned, I had a lot of catching up to do at work---and preparation for our July departure. I was exhausted from a busy day, enjoying the peace and quiet. As I lay swinging in the hammock we had slung from fore to aft in the living area, I heard with dismay the tell-tale sound of paddles quietly breaking the surface of the water, a canoe banging softly against the side of our boat. I had visitors.

I reluctantly extracted myself from the hammock, and went to welcome them. Despite my disappointment at having my peaceful evening disturbed, I couldn't help marveling yet again at the ease with which the local folk could maneuver on the water. One woman of perhaps 45 agilely launched herself from her tippy canoe up through the narrow doorway of BBII. She was followed immediately by a younger woman with a six year old daughter.

The older woman had a gaunt appearance, with protruding lower teeth and several upper teeth missing. I recognized her as the woman who lived with the headman, Pak Thamrin. She quickly told me her name, Aisa, and explained that she was Pak Thamrin's older sister. As their visit wore on, I came to realize that she did not have a shy bone in her body. She was gutsy and bold and very unusual.

Neither she nor Thamrin had ever married---an extremely unusual state of affairs in this area. She was refreshingly frank with me, expressing all her wishes in a most straightforward way. And she was insatiably curious about everything. Over the period of our acquaintance, she wanted to see all my photographs, to look through whatever books I had with pictures or with Indonesian text, to hear about my family and my life. Her laughter filled the boat and my heart with good cheer.

Aisa came that night with Juli, her younger sister, in search of medicine. Another younger brother in law had night blindness. They explained that this was a particular problem for him because he wanted to catch *ulang uli*, and this can only be done at night. He can't afford a powerful enough flashlight to overcome the darkness sufficiently. I gave them 'Alan's multiple vitamins (which he had rejected when the heat and humidity changed their color and odor for the worse). They contained some Vitamin A, and I hoped they might help.

The father of Juli's six year old had left when Juli was still pregnant, and had never come back. I asked about the bandage on the little girl's hand: She had burned her hand on boiling water. They asked about remedies for their sister's cough and shortness of breath. The doctor had told them it was not TB. I didn't know what it could be. I was again reminded of these people's continual health problems and how rare was any medical knowledge or supplies.

During our conversation, Aisa's attention was drawn to a shiny fishing lure, a spoon, that my husband had hooked into the upper bulkhead. She asked to see it, and was obviously delighted with this unusual bit of fishing gear. When she asked for it, I had to tell her sadly that it belonged to my husband, so I couldn't give it away. I'd have to ask him first.

This visit was to be the first of many during the next two months. I gradually learned that the small village of Bukit Tekenang---only about fifteen families---was a *de facto* retreat for the atypical. I had heard before moving there, that the nearby hill from which the village got its name was considered haunted. It was also odd in straddling the border between two *kecamatan* (counties); in having inhabitants originally from several larger villages; and in having almost no resident children. I sometimes wondered if perhaps this village was a last refuge.

Thamrin, who was the headman, was a quiet, reserved man who had never married and continued to live with his never-married sister. Across the water was a couple who had lost all of their children, one by one, to sickness. They had moved to Bukit Tekenang to forget, their home village full of daily reminders of their dead children. Down toward the end of the village lived a mute man; a few doors down from him was a man with the symptoms of leprosy. One of the most taciturn Indonesians I have ever met lived there, a fifty year old man who could perform amazing acrobatic feats, once entertaining my husband at length by standing on his head and turning somersaults in his canoe for an extended period of time!

On a subsequent visit, Aisa told me about a happy dream in which the shiny fishing lure had been hers. I was grateful when my husband agreed to give it to her. In fact, when he saw how pleased she was with the gift, he produced a variety of other fishing equipment he no longer used---line, weights, hooks large and small---and let her and her cohorts take what they liked. Few of our gifts produced such obvious delight.

Our neighbors were all fascinated and pleased with 'Alan's interest in fishing. When I came back from the US, I discovered that Mat Tahar, our "landlord" and the project's handyman, was making 'Alan a castnet. Iwan, a young man living just across the river, had made him a cage of rattan and fishnet in which to keep the *anak toman (Channa Micropeltes* fingerlings) 'Alan was raising as a business venture---the nearest local equivalent to a lemonade stand. That night, Aisa gave him a lecture on how to catch the stickery *ikan patik (Mystus nemurus*) without getting hurt.

Another favorite castoff that our neighbors valued highly was empty glass bottles. All things being equal, we like to have a glass of wine or beer of an evening. Wine was completely unavailable; and we had no refrigeration for beer, which we could buy. We were also embarrassed to be drinking a bottle a day of something considered so expensive by our neighbors. It cost $1.50---a reasonable day's wages for most people there. As a compromise we switched to the much cheaper jenever. Jenever is a Dutch liquor similar to gin, which cost the same price as beer, but lasted us a whole week.

The jenever bottles were much in demand for water storage containers. They had plastic stoppers which could be re-sealed. Aisa was most diligent in getting her share of the jenever bottles we emptied. In return one day, she brought one back to us full of honey. She and her brother had collected it from special bee-hive boards (*tikung*) they set out every year. The bees come every December or January to build their nests among the flowering bushes of the lakes area, and local people provide these boards in which the bees build their hives.

Although we sometimes got tired of Aisa's straightforward requests, she always brought laughter with her. A few days after her gift of honey, she came with a friend who explained that honey was good for *sakit urat*. They looked meaningfully at Dudley. This is a locally defined ailment having to do with the nerves and blood vessels; but, they explained with much hilarity, honey is also good if your husband suffers from impotence. Despite the inapplicability of this ailment in my husband's case, he turned bright red---not entirely used to such earthy humor at his own expense. Aisa's happy, affectionate nature entertained and cheered us. Her sharp mind and insightful comments also helped me to understand the community in which I lived.

Honey in the Forest

In the fall when we had moved to Pulau Majang, my friend, Pak Mu'in, recommended a young man, An, as a possible candidate for our Field Center Manager. An had graduated from high school, and this qualified him as "highly educated" by local standards. We interviewed An and not long after, hired him as a speedboat driver.

He was intelligent and capable and he knew the routes among the bushy trees of the lakes in the northwest corner of the reserve--a nice complement to the skills of our senior driver who came from Jongkong and was more familiar with the southeast. But An was definitely a mixed blessing. His silly giggling drove us crazy, and we were often irritated by his obvious feeling that he was "above" handling fish---as was needed in some of my husband's studies. As time went on, the growing antagonism between this more educated youth from Pulau

Majang and Markan, his older, more experienced boss from Jongkong, became obvious.

I had been hearing local people talk about honey off and on all year, and had planned to study it myself. I knew that somehow people derived income from producing or gathering honey, and I wanted to know more about it. Might it be---with improvements---a way for local people to make a little more money, without harming their environment? I'd read a study of Borneo forest products that singled out honey as one of a few likely prospects for export.

As luck would have it, we were away during the brief honey season in January, and then I got sick and left in the spring for a couple of months. Before I left in April, I gave An a rough outline of how he might conduct a small study of honey production while I was gone, if he had any spare time. I thought this might also keep him and Markan apart.

When I got back he had conducted interviews with a number of honey harvesters in Pulau Majang and in Bukit Tekenang, covering their honey production over the previous three years. He had also written out a description of the entire process as seen from the point of view of a honey harvester; and he had drawn pictures of the equipment needed for harvesting honey.

All that remained for me was the data analysis and writeup---and the fun part of seeking out a few honeyboards to photograph. On a visit to Pulau Majang one day, we took a detour down one of the human-made and human-maintained aquatic paths through inundated forest. The path, with its tubular qualities caused by the overhanging branches reflected in the blackwater, was only slightly wider than our speedboat. I couldn't help thinking that a canoe would have been a more maneuverable vessel in these tight quarters; and my heart lurched as I imagined meeting someone coming the other way at such high speeds. No one else seemed concerned.

An, whose eyes were used to finding honeyboards in among the tree branches, spotted them long before I could make them out. When I failed to see them, he would stop the boat, and the bubbling, boiling blackwater which normally made a tea-colored wake behind us would catch up, embroiling us, as our boat settled in the churning waters created by our engine. Still I had trouble discerning the rectangular honeyboards from the multitudinous branches of these bushy trees. An---ever eager to please---would move us closer and closer to the honeyboard, sometimes miring us hopelessly in among the closely spaced trees.

We made this trip with two young Indonesian scientists who had recently joined our staff, Ali and Heri. As we looked at what still seemed to me a mishmash of unknown greenery, Ali and Heri identified many of the trees; and An gave their local names: *Ketahun (Carallia bracteata*) and *kemensiak (Mesua hexapetalum*) are good trees for supporting the honeyboards. Flowering trees that draw the bees include *mentangis (Ixora mentangis), kebesi (Memecylon edule), kemelayak (Croton cf. ensifolius), ubah (Eugenia sp.), kawi (Shorea balangeran*), and *jijap (Eugenia sp*.). The bees' favorite flowers come from the *ketahun (Garcinia sp*.) and *memasung (Eugenia sp*.) trees, finishing off the season with the most common of all: *Putat (Barringtonia acutangula*). The honeyboards themselves were made of the durable and valuable *tembesu' (Fragraea fragrans*), widely used for house construction by local people.

We came home a roundabout way, going east from Pulau Majang, and swinging southeast across Danau Sentarum (the lake for which the reserve is named). I wondered idly if we should whistle or not. Local people always told us that if we whistled while crossing nearby Lake Luar, the wind would come up. We had a peaceful and beautiful ride back, with the bright blue sky dotted with puffy white clouds. On a shortcut from Danau Sentarum to the Tawang River from the Northeast, we came across a *cin cin apai (Sterna albifrons*, or Little Tern) seated happily on a floating log. We approached the bird slowly in the speedboat, and were able to get quite close before it noticed us and took wing. Heri said this bird's arrival was an indication that the dry season was approaching. I thought how nice it was finally to have some people trained in wildlife and botany with us. We stopped a few more times to look at some of Bukit Tekenang's honeyboards, which were much more accessible. Or maybe I had just gained a little skill in differentiating honeyboards from tree branches!

An's successful accomplishment of a scientific study, almost completely on his own, helped to confirm our growing conviction that village people were a vastly under-utilized human resource. When we started our project in May 1992, we expected to be joined quickly by many other outsiders. For a full year, they did not come; we relied almost exclusively on local people. We found many with useful skills and even more who were capable of learning useful skills with only a modicum of help from us. We concluded that working with and helping train local people in the skills needed for conservation was in fact the most direct way to accomplish conservation goals. People brought in from outside would take their newly acquired skills and leave, whereas local people had built their lives there. Most would remain.

Amoi and the Floating Gardens

Amoi was only about 16 years old, and had quit school before completing 6th grade. To attend school she had to stay in Selimbau, the larger village on the Kapuas where many of Bukit Tekenang's inhabitants had roots and relatives. But she missed her mother too much and quit school to come home to Bukit Tekenang.

When Ida left Bukit Tekenang to return to Jongkong where her father lived, Amoi took over washing our laundry. 'Alan had more or less adopted Amoi's family, while I was in the US; and she had begun to work at the Field Center, helping Yanti, our over-worked and capable young household manager.

I got interested in the floating gardens that were obvious near many of Bukit Tekenang's raft homes. Could these floating gardens be expanded to provide better nutrition to these people who subsisted primarily on fish and rice? There were plenty of indicators of widespread vitamin deficiency: Night blindness, cracking lips, dry skin, anemia, pot bellied children, and high infant mortality. Vegetable produce brought a good price if one chose to sell it; and it didn't seem likely to cause any obvious environmental problems.

I had already looked at the normal, but small terrestrial gardens in Ng. Pengembung. Most women there had a small garden of roughly 100 square meters, on which they grew mainly longbean, cassava, and squash. The fatal flaw with their gardens was the unpredictable timing of the rains. In October 1992, after land preparation, planting, and weeding---just as they were beginning to harvest a few crops---the rains came, and flooded out all the gardens. This was not an uncommon occurrence.

Floating gardens seemed a possible way to obviate this problem. Such gardens rose and fell with the waters. But how many people had them? And what were they growing on them? Again, I'd wanted to study this topic myself; I'd made a few tentative inquiries in Ng. Pengembung (where Sahar had become a full time, salaried assistant), but there were very few of these gardens there. Just before we left for good at the end of June, on a whim I asked the youthful Amoi if she would like to help me. I gave her a questionnaire that I had pretested on a couple of women; and I asked her to interview all the women in Bukit Tekenang who had floating gardens. A little shy at first, it quickly became clear that she was proud to be asked, and she wanted to do a good job. She hesitantly brought me the results of her first interview. She'd done as good a job as any new interviewer would! I sent her out again, with a few minor suggestions, and she successfully interviewed all the women in her community.

She found out a whole range of useful information (what crops they planted, how they managed them, who did the work at each stage of plant growth, whether or not they sold their produce)---enough to make a nice little preliminary report on the topic and to recommend that the idea be further investigated in cooperation with someone trained in horticultural science.

Like Sahar and An and a number of other local people, Amoi helped strengthen my growing conviction that the key to "Third World Development" or "Sustainable Agriculture" or "Conservation" lies with the rural people themselves. There is no limit to what they can do themselves, with just a little encouragement and support (both moral and financial).

Stresses and Strains in the Field Center

By late May, the Field Center was full to overflowing. Ali and Heri had joined us, from Tanjung Pura University in Pontianak; the Conservation Agency had sent up another full time staff member; Enis and Priyo had come from TLI; and we had three college students from Bandung. The Field Center's six bedrooms were full and the ambience was reminiscent of a college dormitory.

One night soon after Ali and Heri joined us, Dudley and I were lying in bed, waiting for the Field Center generator to go off. It was located on the project's raft only a few meters from our boats. The standard operating procedure had been to turn it off at 9 PM. This was so that everyone (especially the villagers and us) could get needed sleep and also to reduce the wear and tear on a machine for which spare parts were two days away. Although I had managed to drift off to sleep---being unusually clever at this activity---Dudley lay there for a full two hours with the generator roaring in his ears before he got sufficiently irritated to get out of bed and investigate.

During the time it took him to put on his clothes in the dark, get into his canoe, paddle it over to the raft and walk up to the Field Center, he managed to get quite angry. Why were these young people keeping everyone awake? They were probably just playing around. What did they think this was, a resort? And so on.

He burst into the main sitting area, which was indeed full of young people, and berated them for keeping everyone awake and leaving the generator on when they knew people were trying to sleep. He stormed out, back down the walkway to the raft and turned off the generator. When he got back into bed, he told me what had happened and expressed the thought that maybe he'd over-reacted a bit. He realized, after the fact, that they were actually studying.

The next morning I was greeted by a very angry Heri, who asked to talk with me. His message was basically that they would not be treated like that, that they had not known about the normal time for turning off the generator, and that they needed and wanted to continue working into the night. I tried to soothe him by explaining that my husband hadn't meant to offend them, that he was just very tired and hadn't understood why the generator did not go off as usual. Besides, he was from New York and New Yorkers were often a little more *keras* (hard, harsh) than other people.

Soon Ali joined us. He was even more upset, hardly willing even to speak. Again I explained, and I apologized. Dudley joined us. He too explained and apologized, saying that he had acted hastily, unwisely and from fatigue. They said they were considering leaving the project because of this. Our words of regret seemed to be having little effect.

At this point, the poignancy of the situation overwhelmed me. We finally had the co-workers we had wanted, and these two were unusually fine people. But difficulties caused by fatigue and cross-cultural miscommunication were threatening to ruin it all. Tears filled my eyes. I could understand their point of view. Indonesians tend to be quite careful of other people's feelings, so my husband's behaviour must have seemed much more extreme to them than it would have to other Americans.

My heart went out to my husband as well who had really meant no harm. He had just been tired and irritated and acted on his irritation. He certainly hadn't expected to precipitate a crisis of this proportion. We were very very happy to have these two motivated, intelligent and hardworking young men. The last thing we wanted to do was drive them away, by accident. My tears seemed to convince them that we actually were genuinely contrite, and they began slowly to forgive us.

We continued to talk for quite a while, and the problem continued to be discussed throughout the day. But Ali and Heri didn't leave. And we bought pressure lamps so that anyone who wanted to study into the night could do so.

Love in the Field Center

It wasn't long after the arrival of the students from Bandung that everyone began to notice that a certain affection seemed to be developing between Titi, one of the students, and our Office Manager,

Luat. They were spending whatever free time they had together, to the delight of most of us who enjoyed having a little romance in our midst.

But one evening Dudley and I were relaxing in our boats when we heard the familiar sound of a canoe approaching. Two of the older men of Bukit Tekenang respectfully asked if they could disturb us, and upon receiving our welcome, climbed into our boat. We were curious as to why they had come, since there was something official about the way they were behaving.

After a bit of chit chat, they got to the point of their visit. Community members had seen Luat and Titi going out alone in a canoe, even after dark. This was against local custom, and they felt it set a bad example for their youth. In fact, they said, if couples were found doing that, community members could force them to marry or beat up on them with impunity.

We were quite surprised (and secretly amused) by this. We wondered if we could go out alone. O, of course, it was fine if married people went out alone. We asked, would there be problems if unmarried people went out in canoes alone in the course of their work? Such work seemed quite likely to be necessary given the mixed gender composition of our team. No, they reassured us, it was only unmarried, romantic outings which were prohibited. We promised to do our best to solve the problem.

It fell to me to discuss this with Luat (he being the more permanent team member). Luat is a Dayak, and Dayaks tend to have much more relaxed attitudes about mingling with the opposite sex than do Melayus. I told him that I personally had no problem whatsoever with his romantic leanings, but that he would have to be more circumspect in his practice, since this was apparently rather strongly disapproved of by our neighbours. His handsome face twisted into an amused grin. That he found the complaint somewhat amusing was a relief to me, as I had no wish to alienate this excellent worker and dear friend. He promised to be more circumspect, and we had no further complaints.

Umping Invites me to the Gawa'

The previous October, I had met and begun working with another anthropologist, Reed Wadley, who was living among the Iban of Wong Garai just outside the northeastern boundary of the reserve. He introduced me to a man who would subsequently become his blood brother: Umping.

Umping was in his early 40's and full of energy, eyes sparkling with intelligence and humor. He was a leader in the regional Iban community, having even served on the People's Representative Council in Putussibau for several years. He was curious about everything, and we quickly got into a serious discussion of development issues in the area---lightened, at periodic intervals, by his quick wit. I explained our project's goals; and I learned of his active role in timber harvesting. I liked him, and continued to enjoy my contacts with him throughout the year.

When I returned from the US in late May, Umping and Reed invited me (and other project staff) to the *Gawa'* at Wong Garai. I had heard about these *Gawa'* since my first visit to DSWR. After their harvest, Iban longhouses hold a shindig---which Reed called a combination between a propitiary ritual and a binge---to which they invite friends and relatives from other longhouses. Indeed this was the "ceremony" to which we had tried to go in Melapi the previous May. The people of nearby Lanjak had also invited me to one in early June of 1992, and I had been disappointed not to be able to attend. So this new invitation was received with considerable anticipation on my part. It would be doubly interesting to me because Umping's daughter was getting married the day after. They would hold both a traditional Iban and a Christian ceremony.

I did however have a few misgivings about how my fellow staff members might react. I knew that the Iban enjoy drinking *arak, tuak*, and *ai' ijuk*, alcoholic drinks forbidden to Muslims---and I knew that a *gawa'* would almost certainly be a time marked by a certain amount of drunken revelry. Iban behavior when drunk, though somewhat different, would not be offensive to most Americans; but I thought it might be to my Muslim co-workers.

The fact that pigs would almost certainly be killed and eaten at the *gawa'* was another feature not likely to endear the Iban community to my co-workers. Still, I reasoned, they have to get used to these cultural differences and develop some tolerance, if we are going to incorporate the Iban---as planned---into our conservation activities. Besides, several co-workers wanted to go, and ....we'd just have to see what happened.

I did, however, take the precaution of bringing the matter up with Reed. As we both well knew, if my friends behaved badly in Iban eyes, it could reflect badly on him, if he hadn't sufficiently distanced himself from my co-workers. Besides his personal ties to his Iban hosts, he had almost another year of research to complete toward his doctorate. We both knew the history of dislike between Muslims and Christians, and among ethnic groups, in Borneo.

Getting Salai

Much to my relief---in an area where communications are extremely difficult and plans regularly change without notice---we got word in mid-June that we should be in Wong Garai on the 26th of June for the *gawa'*. Then began the eternal, "behind the scenes" manipulations among the project staff about who would be accompanying me. The speedboat almost never managed to go anywhere with fewer than its maximum number of passengers.

I said simply that 'Alan and I were going. I also invited Luat (our Maloh Dayak office manager) since he was from the area. *Gawa'*, as well as alcohol and pigs, were part of his own cultural tradition, and I figured he would enjoy it more than most.

On the 25th I began my search for *salai*. *Salai* is the locally made, less-than-delicious, smoked fish we encountered on one of our first visits to the lakes. It can be made from several different kinds of fish. Some of the most popular are *patik (Mystus nemurus*), *landin (M. nigriceps*), and *lais* (including *Kryptopterus sp., Ompok sp., Ceratoglanis scleronema*). Although neither Dudley, 'Alan, nor I ever developed much of a taste for *salai*, it is considered a great delicacy locally; and it's quite expensive by local standards: About $3.00/kg.

I knew that a gift of *salai*---basically a Melayu product---would be very welcome at the Wong Garai festivities. I wanted to be generous to show my appreciation for their acceptance of me---and my nosy anthropological questions---over the year. An and I went first to Ng. Pengembung where *salai* is almost continually being produced. To our great surprise and dismay, they didn't have any! We visited all the tiny settlements in our immediate vicinity. No one seemed to have any, though one family promised a little the next day. Empty-handed, we returned to Bukit Tekenang, where Amoi's father, Mat Tahar, promised us two kilo's the next morning. But this still wouldn't be enough. I figured I needed at least six kilos!

The next morning, I learned who besides 'Alan and Luat would be joining me on this outing. Markan would drive the speedboat; Enis wanted to add to her fish collection; and Heri would bring along the new project videocorder to tape the proceedings. We picked up our two kilo's of *salai* from Mat Tahar, and headed for Ng. Pengembung. There the folks had managed to produce another two kilo's, but we were still short. We would try the other small communities we would pass along the way. Someone might have some.

The day was beautiful. The early morning sun had not yet acquired the heat of mid-day, and the blue sky again was studded with lovely white clouds. My Indonesian co-workers huddled down in their coats against the morning chill, while 'Alan and I---used to a temperate clime---enjoyed the cooling breeze made by the speedboat's passage through the water. Heri, much enamored of the new videocorder, spent half his time sitting on the gunwale "hunting" and "shooting" the flora and fauna.

We first crossed Danau Sentarum, then following a series of small rivers, we crossed still more lakes. We were surprised that the waters were still as high as they were. I remembered going to Badau the previous June, when the trip had been stretched to five hours each way, by the low water level.

I was just beginning to get concerned again about our acquisition of more *salai* when we came across a Melayu *motor*---like our home, only smaller. Markan pulled up and attached the speedboat to the *motor*, inquiring if they had any *salai*. Luck was with us. They did.

We were invited inside. As usual, I bent double going through the door at the bow, and sat cross-legged on the floor. I could see the eyes of both husband and wife open wide, with the common combination of interest and fear when confronted at close quarters with a strange and, in their view, large, western woman.

It took them a while to get up their courage to explain to me that they had three kinds of *salai*, each a different price. Which did I prefer? The man began pulling up his floorboards. We looked down into the hold of the boat, and found baskets and baskets of dried fish. He pulled out samples of the various kinds to show us, assuming more knowledge than I possessed about their relative merits and demerits. With a little expert advice from Luat, we finally decided to take a little of each.

While the husband took the scale down from its hook on the ceiling and got it ready to weigh the *salai*, Markan---who seemed to know everyone in the entire lakes area---reminded him of their relationship, and urged him not to charge me too high a price. I personally didn't think he would have dared anyway! Happy to find sufficient quantities, I decided to be really generous. I bought six more kilos.

When I had paid my money and received my bags of *salai*, I again bent double to exit, and experienced the always delightful relief of being able to straighten out my 5' 5" body length on the foredeck. By the time we left, the couple had decided that we were indeed human, and did not present any direct threat to their well-being. For that matter, we had proved to be a significant profit for the day. We were sent on our way with smiles and enthusiastic waves.

But we were not finished dealing with this *salai*. We were going to have to get it up a small mountain---all ten kilo's of it!---from the large village of Lanjak (the *kecamatan* capital) to the longhouse of Wong Garai. We had been told that Umping would have a truck waiting for us to take us up the frightening and precipitous road that links Wong

Garai to Lanjak and the lakes. I wasn't sure I was disappointed when the truck did not materialize.

I had been up and down that road several ways: on foot, by log truck, by mini-bus, and by motorcycle. The latter was definitely my preferred mode of transport, but we obviously couldn't all fit on a motorcycle. I considered the idea of using my advanced age as an excuse to ride a motorcycle. It would have been easy to tap into the perhaps pan-Indonesian custom of babying older, foreign women. I reluctantly rejected this idea. Heck, there wasn't one available anyway. My second choice was walking---though even this had been a rather horrendous experience.

Reed had accompanied me on my first visit to Wong Garai the previous October. He was in his early thirties and in excellent shape. I had just met him, so was embarrassed to ask him to slow down as we began our second hour hiking at a fast clip up the steep mountain under the noonday sun.

Struggling to keep up with him, trying to keep my heavy breathing quiet, my heart fell as he cheerfully told me how he had been able to hold his own, walking with his Iban hosts. The Iban are famous as great walkers. Among the Melayu, anyone walking fast or able to walk great distances is likened to an Iban. I myself had fallen fifteen minutes behind a skinny tubercular Iban woman of my own age on my first visit to Empaik, in what proved to be a half hour walk for me.

While our mode of transport was being discussed, Markan was also trying to decide whether he wanted to accompany us or not. Pretending concern about leaving the speedboat unattended, I had the distinct impression he was really afraid to come along.

In the end we wound up walking up the mountain. Fortunately the hour was earlier, and my companions less accomplished walkers, making the trip a little less strenuous than my October visit had been. We actually enjoyed much of the two hour walk, with Heri entertaining us with his videomaking whenever we tired of conversation.

As we neared our destination, a large, rickety truck full of standing people swayed to a stop near us and offered us a ride. The passengers could not believe it when I politely declined, saying I was afraid to ride on the truck. A Westerner, afraid of a truck, when they knew I walked the forests of Kalimantan alone and (usually) unafraid. How strange!

The *salai*, shared out among us on the long trek up the hill, was received most gratefully by our hosts, and promptly divided with friends and relatives from other longhouse apartments. I think the other members of our party even enjoyed eating some of it.

The Gawa' at Wong Garai

Reed had been living among the Iban for over a year at this point; and his Iban family and he had decided that he should participate actively in his household's *gawa'*, including acting as a host. This entailed, among other things, a pig being slaughtered on his behalf, wearing traditional Iban attire, and learning some Iban ceremonial prayers and their accompanying rituals.

By the time we arrived about ten, the longhouse had already been celebrating for a number of hours. A long awaited cockfight, on which longhouse members and visitors alike placed bets, had just concluded; and the alcoholic libations were flowing freely. We were greeted enthusiastically, and taken down the length of the longhouse, past three apartments which were holding big *gawa*'s. One man walked around the decorated post in front of each of these apartments, continually chanting Iban prayers. He was followed by two other men who chanted a refrain. They did this all day and all night; and the bigger the *gawa'* the more days and nights they kept it up. I still marvel, wondering how on earth they managed to stay on their feet. One's gratitude for good fortune determines the size of the *gawa'* one puts on.

At Umping's apartment, we were offered fresh, delicious---and alcoholic---*ai' ijuk*, the "water of the palm." As the day wore on, we witnessed many interesting traditions. I was, with difficulty, dressed in traditional Iban garb---a straight, brightly decorated skirt, covered at the waist with a silver belt. Around my neck and chest hung a huge and beautiful silver necklace. I joined about eight lovely young women, similarly attired, carrying out plates of artistically arranged eggs and sticky rice for the ancestor gods (the leftovers could be eaten by the men seated on the front porch). Being at least twice as big and twice as old as my serving companions, I felt a little ridiculous, but they seemed pleased. Much to my chagrin, Heri's videocorder was rolling the whole time!

Shortly after these foods were arranged beautifully in front of the men (many of whom bore elaborate and beautiful tattoos), each family killed a pig. The pig's liver was immediately extracted from the dead pig, and brought first to the old men to examine. The liver was then passed around for everyone to see. These special pig livers were believed to hold hints about the future. According to Reed's pig liver, he would return to the US and overcome all obstacles; and/or he would soon return to Wong Garai after visiting the US; and/or he would return to Wong Garai from the US and marry his neighbor's daughter!

By the time Reed had to do his ceremonial prayers as a *gawa'* host, he was--perhaps mercifully—three sheets to the wind. His family stripped him to his undershorts, and wound the elaborate Iban *sirat* (loincloth) around his starkly white skin. He looked quite impressive in Iban attire, holding a chicken under his arm and saying I knew not what. Although I did not know enough to be sure, he seemed to do a marvelous job of pounding a spear, throwing rice into the air, and chanting Iban prayers to the spirits. I later learned he was actually just holding onto the spear---probably for support, in his condition!

After this ritual, we were told we must begin a difficult (but required) trip back up the length of the longhouse, stopping at each apartment and drinking *tuak* with each host. A group of young men took some of the pigs out beyond the longhouse to a spit, and began roasting it. I joined them, to escape the constant chatter and curiosity of my hosts (and to reduce my alcohol consumption).

One end of the Wong Garai longhouse is on the road; but if you go to the other end, and descend the notched log that serves as steps, you enter a cool orchard with a path winding through it. Following the path, you soon reach a stream (the Sedik River) which has a beautiful, clear pool of water. Surrounded by rocks partially submerged in swiftly running water, you can immerse yourself in the calmer pool. What utter delight it had been the previous October when I first found this beautiful pool of cool water, after walking up that mountain in the heat of the sun, sweat dripping off my body, smelling like a horse. Heaven! And it was such a nice surprise to find water that was not the color of tea and was safe to drink. A little further along is a beautiful waterfall in an area which the longhouse is protecting as a forest reserve.

To get to the barbecuing pigs, I traversed the pool and a fast-moving feeder stream, and found several young men eager to feed me tender morsels of newly roasted and delicious pig. They themselves considered the brain wrapped in a banana leaf and the ears to be especially delicious. I was satisfied with the regular meat myself. I stayed out in this picnic-like setting as long as I could, reluctantly returning to the party as darkness fell, when the young men finished their cooking.

Remaining sober is not an easy thing at a *gawa'*. Indeed, in some Iban longhouses, lovely young maidens actually gang up on visitors, holding them down while they forcibly pour *tuak* down their throats. Even in Wong Garai, where only social pressure was brought to bear, refusal was difficult. Reed was able to protect me a little; my Muslim co-workers could plead religious aversion; but poor Reed had no acceptable excuse. As the afternoon wore on, he became drunker and drunker.

Heri, Markan and Enis (my Muslim co-workers) actually displayed remarkable equanimity throughout this day, which was certainly alien and probably distressing to them. But when it became clear that we would continue drinking far into the night, they decided they must leave. They had survived the pig killing, managed to withstand the beginnings of the drinking, but I guess the idea of a whole longhouse of drunken Dayaks was too much for them.

However, deciding to leave was to prove much easier than actually doing so. Umping took me aside and explained that it was bad form for guests at a *gawa'* to leave at night. They were supposed to stay till the next morning. Reed, by now quite beyond the pale, joined in, urging them to stay, holding onto their arms, telling them they would be offending their hosts, and so on. This went on for quite some time, until I felt compelled to intervene. I suggested a trade: That 'Alan, Luat and I would stay, but that the other three really had to go, that "duty called" at Bukit Tekenang. This compromise was reluctantly accepted. Markan, Heri and Enis left, and Luat and I continued the fight to moderate our liquor consumption until we could finally slip off to bed about 3 in the morning!

Throughout all this, Umping moved unobtrusively, making sure everyone had food and drink, that the young rowdies were not getting out of hand, making everyone feel welcome. He was available if needed as Reed played the new role of *gawa'* host. He even took time out from planning for his daughter's wedding the next day to chat with me about politics over a meal in his kitchen. The next December, when I wrote and told him that my father was dying of cancer, he wrote to tell me how sorry he was and that his household would hold a special prayer at Christmastime. Against so many odds, we were able to establish a warm bond of friendship that will stay with me always.

Chapter VI: Farewell to the People of DSWR

By springtime, we had begun to have serious questions in our own minds about whether we should stay on at DSWR. We were extremely pleased with the progress we had made with local people. Their interest, enthusiasm and talents were a constant delight for us. But the bureaucratic problems showed no signs of abating. Unrealized plans, unapproved budgets, failure to get project funds to the province or even our salary checks to our bank, along with a myriad other problems continued to plague us. Probably the biggest factor for me was my feeling that those holding the purse strings (ODA, SCF, and LTI) neither trusted nor cared about us. The difficult living conditions were a minor inconvenience, and would have been well worth enduring if other elements in the project had been proceeding as we hoped. In March we gave notice with a strong qualifications. We said if things improved, we would love to stay. Although many promises were made about improvements that would be forthcoming, by May, we reluctantly realized that nothing was going to change. We came to the conclusion that, for us in this project, the negatives outweighed the positives. We decided that our notice would stand. We would leave.

A Few Private Goodbyes

I knew when I left Wong Garai after the *Gawa'* that I wouldn't be back for quite a long time. My family and I were leaving the Wildlife Reserve, leaving the Conservation Project---with great sadness. I told the people I knew well in Wong Garai how happy I was that I had the chance to get to know them, and how much I appreciated their accepting me as they had.

I tried hard to convey to all our friends our personal sadness at leaving. The sorrow one always feels when leaving people one has come to care about was multiplied in this case by my sense that working with these people was the right way to go. I saw how much we could accomplish with them, and I was afraid that those who followed us would not know or understand the potential these people represented.

A few days later, I went to pick up 'Alan who had stayed a couple of nights with Habiba's family in Ng. Pengembung, for the last time. Habiba was sitting quietly with her husband inside her tiny raft, with tear-filled eyes. She told me that 'Alan was like her own child, and she couldn't bear for him to leave. Couldn't I just leave him there with her? She could take good care of him and see that he got an education. She knew of course that was impossible. I took pictures of everyone together, and promised to try to bring him back. What else could I do? But we all knew that even if I could bring him back, a visit would never be the same as having each other as neighbors.

On one of the last evenings before we left, I was relaxing in our open door, keeping an open eye for the three Pied Hornbills (*Anthrococeros coronatus*) that often flew by at dusk. I had been trying to get a picture of them for weeks, and had not yet succeeded in having the enhanced telescopic lens on the camera at quite the perfect moment.

Watching for the hornbills, I didn't notice the approach of canoes. When we heard the canoes bumping the sides of our boat, we correctly surmised that Pak Sahar and Pak Sa'id were coming with their wives and children to say goodbye. They all solemnly entered our living room, and sat quietly for a moment. Then Pak Sahar began to cry. He told how much it had meant to him to work with us, that he had learned so much, and that he believed in what we had been trying to do. He was so sorry we were leaving, and he would miss us so much. He hoped that we all had long life so that we could meet again sometime. It was impossible not to cry.

As so often happens in Indonesian villages (probably in any poor village), a plan to move signals, besides sadness, an interest in what will become of the mover's belongings. I was not surprised when our neighbors began making visits to find out what we were taking and what we were leaving, and to let us know which things they themselves might like. Amoi's mother wanted one of my shirts. Aisa wanted my tennis shoes to protect her feet from the spines of rattan while harvesting during the coming dry season. Children came, asking for

'Alan's comic books, his clothes, any toys he might be willing to part with.

Some things we selected for special people. I wanted Habiba to have my small stove-top oven and cake tins; my husband wanted to give his tools to Sa'id; 'Alan's small canoe went to his friend, Beli. We all divested ourselves of nearly all the clothing we had brought upriver.

In the end, I decided to bring everything remaining, to the Field Center at our goodbye party. I would simply hand it out like Santa Claus, one by one to those expressing an interest in it. I figured that in this way community pressure would ensure more fairness than we could manage on our own. Compared to other experiences leaving Indonesian villages, this strategy worked pretty well.

A Melayu Good Bye Party

The party, on the night before we left, drew everyone from the community and all our co-workers. Community members began assembling in the early evening, first to watch Ali's and Heri's latest video attempts. These amateur producers had managed to get incredible footage from one of the project boats of a snake, racing across the surface of the water and making attack motions toward the boat. They did lovely videos---as yet unedited---of DSWR scenery, wildlife, local communities, fishing activities. And all were popular with the local community.

After the video's, we distributed what we were leaving behind; and then the fun began. The men clustered at one end, and the women at the other. The women were by far the rowdier, vying to sit by me, hug me, and generally express their affection. They envied my "beautiful white skin," they thought my husband was handsome, they wanted my son (who had fallen asleep, exhausted) to come out and be photographed with them. Horsing around, they repeatedly unwound the elderly Ma' Kedebu's hair; they lay their legs out next to mine to compare size and color.

Pak Kedebu' (a nickname meaning "Mr. *Oxyeleotris marmorata*," an expensive fish also sometimes called *ikan bodoh*, or "Stupid fish") began to play beautifully on a wooden guitar. He was soon joined by Iwan's father on a "drum" that was simply a wooden box. This was the first artistic event we had seen, among the Melayu. As the men played their rhythmic tunes, a few brave individuals and couples gradually began to dance a traditional dance, one or two at a time. The porch, lighted by the project's generator, became a warm haven in which we were all encircled by friendship and affection, a little mesmerized by the rhythm of the music and the dance. Beyond was the blackness of the night.

The next morning, with heavy hearts, we loaded our remaining goods into one speedboat, and began saying our goodbyes. We took pictures of the project team---larger than it had ever been! We cried some tears.

And then we got into the other speedboat, and slowly circled the village. As we passed each raft, the people came out to wave goodbye, watching until we went around the first bend in the Tawang River. We were out of sight.

A few minutes later we passed Nanga Pengembung. Again, the community came out on the boardwalk and the rafts, and waved goodbye to us. We cried still more tears.

Epilogue Number 1 (1994)

I've had time, during the past year and a half, to contemplate the experience, to think of what it's meant to me and what lessons I've learned from it. It kind of reminds me of another experience I had years ago. My former husband, Michael, and I built a sailboat. He was a purist and a traditionalist when it came to sailing, and our 37' sailboat had no engine. We finished building it in the summer of 1977, and we took it for its (and our) shakedown cruise in Puget Sound. That summer alternated between absolutely idyllic delights and some of the most horrendous experiences I've known. One day we would find ourselves moored in a safe and beautiful harbor, with the warm sun on our backs, eating delicious crabs freshly caught from the clear waters beneath us, drinking a glass of wine and talking with fascinating new friends from a nearby boat. The next, as night fell, we'd be fighting against a falling tide with very little wind, trying to find an anchorage before darkness enveloped us completely. Exhausted and freezing from the wet frigidity of Puget Sound, we would haul out the 12 foot oars, and add our pitiful human muscle to the power of the failing winds.

Danau Sentarum was a bit like that. I was exhausted much of the time---from the physical conditions, the diet, the water, the various stresses and strains. But a whole host of memories delight: Idyllic moments alone on the water, lying on our deck peering at the stars with my husband, sudden surprising insights about people, communication on an unexpectedly deep level, cheerful cooperation among team members. The year, the people, the place will not be forgotten.

During this last year and a half, the project has had one leader who was antagonistic to local people living in the reserve. But he is gone, and Julia, an ODA intern who shares many of my own views about cooperating with local communities, has come. The project, in my mind, is back on track. But the fact remains that problems as mundane as LTI's chaotic bookkeeping, SCF's greed, and ODA's pokey tranfers of money---compounded by a certain arbitrariness in central governmental decisionmaking---wreaked havoc with this attempt to integrate people into an important conservation effort. These constraints to conservation were much more significant and intractable than those provided by local people.

This experience confirmed for me what had been only a suspicion and a hope. I now know that rural people are the secret to their own "development" and to "conservation" of their areas. The role of outsiders like myself must be as a conduit and a catalyst, not as preachers or teachers. If we can get better organized, we should be able to bring resources and additional perspectives; but most fundamentally we must recognize, rely on and build on what already exists in these people's knowledge, organization, and creative energy.

Epilogue Number 2 (2005)

Between 1993 and the present, many changes have occurred in Indonesia and in Danau Sentarum. Indonesia was led by five different presidents between 1998 and 2004 (in contrast to one over the previous 30 years); it has weathered the major Asian economic crisis of 1997-98; and there has been a major governmental decentralization effort, which has resulted in great confusion about authority over natural resources and protected areas. Borneo was particularly hard hit by the 1997-98 El Niño, which caused major fires in East Kalimantan, and dramatic smoke and other problems in West Kalimantan. Large scale ethnic violence hit some areas of West Kalimantan, though it spared the Danau Sentarum area.

The Conservation project itself continued for a few more years, usually with a couple of constantly changing foreign personnel, never attaining the level of official Indonesian government support originally envisioned. Some progress was made in cataloguing the ecological conditions and characteristics of the area, and in developing and marketing several forest products (honey, woven baskets, homemade paper). The area, like most of Indonesia's forested areas, has been the victim of rampant illegal logging; and ever-present plans for major oil palm plantation and transmigration projects, and even damming of the lakes, are still being discussed.

But on a more positive note, the head of Kapuas Hulu *Kabupaten*, in which Danau Sentarum is located, declared his *kabupaten* to be a Conservation District, in 2003.

An, the once-silly young man who began as our boat driver fresh out of high school, has worked on numerous international projects over the intervening years, learning a number of skills, which are now put to use in a local NGO, Riak Bumi. Ida, our laundress, left Danau Sentarum to go to computer school, and worked for me as a data collector on a return visit in 1996. The two founding fathers of Riak Bumi, Valentinus Heri and Adi, also "native sons," began working for the Conservation Project, after we left. The members of this NGO have consistently maintained some level of conservation activity in the rserve, which was re-designated as a National Park in the mid-1990s. They re-activated the *Suara Bakakak* newsletter, and have kept it going. They have applied for and received funds from a number of donors; maintained contacts with the various foreigners who have worked there and who by and large retain their affection and concern for the people and the area; and are now working with the Center for International Forestry Research (CIFOR), on a collaborative project to involve both communities and local government in managing the Park (funded by Ford Foundation and CIFOR). One Riak Bumi member attended The Heart of Borneo conference in the Netherlands, in May 2005, presenting the progress they've made.

My own experience there, which had strengthened my sense of the capabilities of local people to be directly involved in decisionmaking about conservation and development issues, resulted in my leading the development of a new program called Local People, Devolution and Adaptive Collaborative Management of Forests, at CIFOR. This program experimented with community management of local forest resources---emphasizing collaboration among stakeholders and social learning---in 30 sites in 11 countries; and it built on the idea that outsiders should serve as catalysts for local collective action and empowerment. Two of my CIFOR colleagues, Linda Yuliani and Yayan Indriatmoko, are now working closely with the Riak Bumi personnel to apply elements of this approach in Danau Sentarum National Park. One of their early activities was to produce a short film about the conservation dilemmas in Danau Sentarum.

The message I take home from my own experience in Danau Sentarum (and elsewhere) is that issues of conservation and development are part of complex and changing systems---systems that are too complex and dynamic to be planned from outside. The only hope for conservation areas, and it's a realistic hope, is to motivate and allow the people who live there to be very involved---to develop shared or complementary goals, to plan how to reach those goals, to implement plans and monitor what happens, and to work with others (governments, timber companies, conservation agencies/projects) to manage their areas in ways that work. This kind of process is messy---involving many different interests, variable levels of power, and lots of conflict and negotiation. But it's probably the only way that will work. The people who live in conservation areas are there for the long haul; they can do it best. What we outsiders can do is provide support, including confidence in their ability to do so.

Cast of Characters and Organizations

Agus, the short term counterpart from CA's sister agency in Pontianak, met in Pulau Majang

Aisa, the gutsy and curious, unmarried sister of Bukit Tekenang's headman, Pak Thamrin

'Alan, the author's 10 and 11 year old son

Ali, a young Indonesian botanist from Tanjung Pura University (Pontianak) who came in June as a counterpart

Amoi, Mat Tahar's daughter and the Field Center's junior housekeeper; also floating garden researcher

An, our second boat driver, a high school graduate, from Pulau Majang; also honey researcher

Ayu, Guntam's wife and our first "cook" in Ng. Pengembung

Bangkang, the lovely, young wife of Empaik's headman

Beli, Habiba's son and 'Alan's good friend, Ng. Pengembung

Bembang, Injan's bright, 10 year old daughter from Empaik

Brian, Dudley's 21 year old son

Bu Juleha, the proprietress of Pulau Majang's "hotel"

CA, the Indonesian Conservation Agency in Pontianak

Caya, a lovely Iban farmer, from Empaik

Didin, the troublesome CA employee who caused problems in Pulau Majang

Dudley, the author's husband and Chief of Party

Edi, Habiba's son in law and Mboi's jealous husband, Ng. Pengembung

Enis, a young Indonesian fisheries scientist from TLI who participated in our initial trip there and returned after the Field Centre was built

Gillian, 'Alan's 19 year old, American tutor

Guntam, owner of the house where Gillian stayed in Ng. Pengembung and where we dined in the fall

Habiba, the friendly and beautiful grandmother who first lured us to Ng. Pengembung

Haji Idui, aka the "Good Haji," the Selimbau building contractor for the Field Center (in contrast to the land-"owning," "Bad Haji")

Haji Walidat, Markan's patron in Suhaid who built many of our boats

Heri, a young Indonesian wildlife specialist from Tanjung Pura University (Pontianak), who came just before we left, as a counterpart

Hugh, the man investigating living conditions for our proposed volunteer co-workers

Ian, a young, volunteer wildlife biologist who joined us in Pulau Majang for a few weeks in December

Ida, Maimun's high school educated daughter and our first laundress in Bukit Tekenang

Injan, a brave and funny Iban woman from Empaik

Iwan, a young man living on a raft in Bukit Tekenang, 'Alan's fish cage culture "tutor"

Jives, the suave, neo-colonialist team leader at SCF, responsible for funneling project funds from ODA to TLI, Jakarta.

John, the older forester from ODA, member of the Review Team

Juli, Aisa's younger sister, Bukit Tekenang

LTI, Lowland Tropical Institute, an international NGO specializing in wetlands, and responsible for the conservation project in Danau Sentarum Wildlife Reserve.

Luat, the Field Center Office Manager and a Maloh Dayak from the Lanjak area

Ma' Kedebu', an old fisherwoman living on a raft in Bukit Tekenang near the Field Center

Maimun, an intelligent woman from Jongkong, residing on a Bukit Tekenang raft, who baked cookies for sale

Markan, our first boat driver and expert guide, from Jongkong

Mary Jane, the social scientist from ODA, member of the Review Team

Mat Tahar, a Bukit Tekenang resident, the Field Center's handiman, and part owner of the land on which it was built

Mboi, Habiba's 14 year old, married daughter, Ng. Pengembung

Mni', a dumpy, "healthy" Iban matron with a toothache, from Empaik

ODA, Overseas Development Administration (British foreign aid, now Department for International Development, DfID)

Pak Abdulatif, a neighbour in Ng. Pengembung who caught a monitor lizard

Pak Ali, representative of the *camat* in Selimbau

Pak Kedebu', a guitar-playing fisherman living on a raft in Bukit Tekenang near the Field Center

Pak Mu'in, the over-worked, intelligent headman of Pulau Majang

Pak Sahlan, local crocodile expert from Ng. Kenelang.

Pak Thamrin, unmarried, head fisherman at Bukit Tekenang

Pak Tori, the second head of the Indonesian Conservation Agency in Pontianak

Pak Toto, the head of West Kalimantan's Conservation Agency when the project started

Pak Wawan, the intellectual foreman at the Field Center, from Selimbau

Parto, a junior Conservation Agency employee, in charge of our project within the agency.

Polmer, a mid-level Conservation Agency employee

Reed, a doctoral student in anthropology at Arizona State University, living in the Iban longhouse of Wong Garai, also a consultant on the Project

Rimpun, a CA employee who joined us as our first long term counterpart

Sahar, our neighbour in Ng. Pengembung, and a part time employee of the Conservation Project

Sa'id, Sahar's soft-spoken, gentle neighbour and an occasional part time employee of the Conservation Project

SCF, Scottish Consulting Firm, a profit-making firm with which LTI had a sub-contract for the Conservation Project

Steve, the young economist from ODA, member of the Review Team

Telly, the owner of the Istana Kapuas "hotel," Selimbau

Timah, Ng. Pengembung's best gardener (female)

Titi, a college student from Bandung working on her senior thesis at the Field Center

Umping, an intelligent and personable leader in the Iban community of Wong Garai

Wim, the casual, TLI ecologist in charge of the Conservation Project at Danau Sentarum Wildlife Reserve, Bogor.

Yanti, the Field Center's household manager, from Semitau

Glossary*

Local Language	*English*	*Latin or Literal*
ai' ijuk (I)	alcoholic beverage from palms	"water of the palm"
air mati	plain water	"dead water"
air putih	plain water	"white water"
ambai (M)	large dipnet	
anak toman	toman fingerlings	*Channa micropeltes*
arak	bought alcoholic beverage	
Badau	Kec. capitol, NW of DSWR	
bakakak	Stork-billed kingfisher	*Pelargopsis capensis*
bandung	river-going house-shaped ship	
Belitung River	access to DSWR from Kapuas	
betutu'	a fish	*Oxyeleotris marmorata*
bodi terbang	speedboat	
Buaya Biru	Blue Crocodile	
bukit	hill	
Bukit Empaik	hill, NW corner of DSWR	
Bukit Tekenang	hill, center of DSWR, Field Ctr. site	
camat	Chief Executive in a "county"	
cin cin apai	Little Tern	*Sterna albifrons*
danau	lake	
dukun	traditional healer	
Empaik	Iban longhouse, NW corner of DSWR	
gawa' (I)	Harvest Festival	
Genting	tiny Melayu village, Lake Pengembung	
Haji	person who has gone to Mecca	
haram	forbidden by Islam	
Hari Raya	End of Fasting month celebration	"Grand Day"
Iban	a Dayak ethnic group	
ikan	fish	
Ikan bodoh	"stupid fish"	*Oxyeleotris marmorata*
Istana Kapuas	Kapuas Palace "Hotel", Selimbau	
Jasa Kapuas	Kapuas Merit "Hotel", Semitau	
jelawat	a fish, snakehead	*Leptobarbus hoevenii*
jermal (M)	large fishnet, closing off river mouth	
jijap	a tree, popular with bees	*Eugenia sp.*

Jongkong	Kec. capitol, on Kapuas River	
Kabupaten	Regency (above county)	
Kapuas Hulu	Regency in which DSWR is located	
kawi	a tree, popular with bees	*Shorea balangeran*
kayu	wood	
kebesi	a tree, popular with bees	*Memecylon edule*
Kecamatan	County	
kedebu'	a fish	*Oxyeleotris marmorata*
kemelayak	a tree, popular with bees	*Croton cf. ensifolius*
kemensiak	a tree, good for placing honeyboards	*Mesua hexapetalum*
keras	harsh, hard	
ketahun	a tree, good for bees and honeyboards	*Carallia bracteata*
lais	a fish, popular for smoking	*Kryptopterus spp., Ompok spp.*
Lake Bekuan	small lake, SE corner of DSWR	
Lake Belida'	small lake, south of Lake Sentarum	
Lake Luar	large lake, NE corner of DSWR	
Lake Sentarum	large lake, northern half of DSWR	aka "Danau Turus Duata"
Lake Seriang	lake, NW corner of DSWR	
landin	a fish, popular for smoking	*Mystus nigriceps*
Lang Buana	Wandering Eagle or Owl	
lanting (M)	a raft, with or without house	
longbot	open motorized small boat	
Majang River	river just East of Pulau Majang	
Maloh	a Dayak ethnic group	
Melayu	Muslim ethnic group	
memasung	a tree, popular with bees	*Eugenia sp.*
mentangis	a tree, popular for firewood and bees	*Ixora mentangis*
monyet Belanda	"Dutch monkey" (for large nose)	*Nasalis larvatus*
motor	medium sized house-shaped boat	
nanga	confluence (of 2 rivers)	
Nanga Empenang	Melayu village on Tawang River	Ng. = abbrev.
Nanga Kenelang	Melayu village on Tawang River	Ng. = abbrev.
Nanga Leboyan	Melayu village, eastern edge, DSWR	Ng. = abbrev.
Nanga Pengembung	small Melayu village on Tawang R.	Ng. = abbrev.
ngamok (M)	to get angry	
Nyibung	small village on Kapuas, nr. Selimbau	
nyamuk	mosquito	

obat	medicine	
obat nyamuk	mosquito repellent/coil/insecticide	
patik	a fish, popular for smoking	*Mystus nemurus*
pulau	island (M), or forest reserve (Iban)	
Pulau Majang	large Melayu village, NW DSWR	
Pulau Melayu	tiny island in Lake Luar, NE DSWR	
propinsi	province	
putat	the most common shrub, popular/bees	*Barringtonia acutangula*
Ramadan	the Muslim holy month of fasting	
ramai	lively, active, sociable, busy	
rancong	Proboscis monkey	*Nasalis larvatus*
Rancong Loncat	Jumping Proboscis	*Nasalis larvatus*
sakit urat	vein/nerve ailment/impotence	
salai	smoked whole fish	
Sedik River	river behind Wong Garai (NE DSWR)	
Sekolat	large village on Belitung R., in DSWR	
Selimbau	Kec. capitol, on Kapuas River	
Semitau	Kec. capitol, on Kapuas River	
sholat	Muslim prayer at dusk	
suara	voice	
Suhaid	large Melayu village on Kapuas River	
sungai	river	
tabung (M)	bamboo fish trap	
Taman	a Dayak ethnic group	
tembesu'	a tree, popular for construction	*Fragraea fragrans*
temenggung (I)	highest Iban traditional leader	
tikung (M)	boards used to attract bees	
tinjau (M)	black and white bird (flycatcher-shrike?)	*Hemipus sp.?*
toman	a fish	*Channa micropeltes*
tuak	alcoholic beverage from rice	
ubah	a tree	*Eugenia sp.*
ulang uli	a fish	*Botia macracanthus*
Wong Garai	Iban longhouse, NE of DSWR	

* M = Melayu
I = Iban

www.ingramcontent.com/pod-product-compliance
Ingram Content Group UK Ltd.
Pitfield, Milton Keynes, MK11 3LW, UK
UKHW041942190726
13854UKWH00004B/1733

9 781411 677593